D0731401

SWEET STITCHES

from the Heart

HILLSBORO PUBLIC LIBRARIES
Hillsboro, OR
Member of Washington County
COOPERATIVE LIBRARY SERVICES

MORE THAN 70 PROJECT IDEAS AND 900 STITCH MOTIFS FOR ANGELS, TEDDIES, FAIRIES, HEARTS, AND ALPHABETS, PLUS ESSENTIAL EMBROIDERY AND CROSS-STITCH TECHNIQUES

SWEET STITCHES
from the Heart

anne sohier-fournel

agnès delage-calvet

isabelle leloup

photography by
frédéric lucano, hiroko mori, and richard boutin

HILLSBORO PUBLIC LIBRARIES
Hillsboro, OR
Member of Washington County
COOPERATIVE LIBRARY SERVICES

new york

Copyright © 2011 by Marabout/Hachette Livre
Translation copyright © 2011 by Potter Craft

All rights reserved.
Published in the United States by Potter Craft, an
imprint of the Crown Publishing Group, a division
of Random House, Inc., New York.
www.crownpublishing.com
www.pottercraft.com

POTTER CRAFT and colophon is a registered
trademark of Random House, Inc.

Much of the material in this work was previously
published in the following titles, all published in
France by Marabout/Hachette Livre, Paris: *Anges,
Fées, Coeurs, Ours, Petits Mots de Filles, Pour Les
Tout-Petits, Mots Tendres au Point du Croix, Mots
Doux au Point de Croix,* and *Jeux de Mots: Au
Point de Croix.*

Library of Congress Catalogue-in-Publication Data
available from the Library of Congress.

ISBN 978-0-307-58688-9

Cover and interior design by veést design
Front cover photography by Hiroko Mori
and Frédéric Lucano (top left)
Translation by Claire Kelley

10 9 8 7 6 5 4 3 2 1

First edition

Printed in China

48239155 3/12

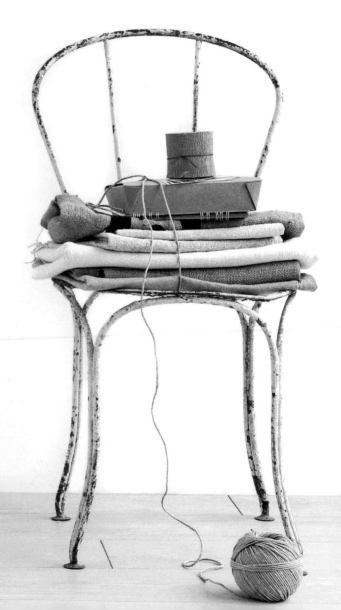

acknowledgments

From Agnès and Anne: Thank you to Christine and her fingers, and to Isabelle for opening the doors of her gorgeous apartment to us. Thanks also to Pascale Chombart de Lauwe, Christine, Hiroko, and Vania, as well as Fred and Dominique.

From Anne: Thanks to our good fairies Pascale and Katrine; to Zoé, Sonia, Fred, Lotta, Soiz, Joséphine; and to my angels Lilas, Maud, and Serj. Thank you to Anne-Marie, Emmanuelle, Hélène, Jean Eudes, Georges, Valou, Françoise Soizic and all the friends who encouraged me. A big thank-you also to Fred and Sonia. Thank you to Serge, my special advisor; thanks also to my girls, to Maria-Eva, and to Fred and Christine for their combined talents. And, last but not least, to Florence and François, who so kindly offered us their apartment.

From Isabelle: My greatest thanks to all my fairy godmothers, my suppliers—for their wonderful linens, shimmering ribbons, amazing buttons, but above all for the laughs we shared, their supportive advice, and the lovely cupcakes. They certainly know how precious they are to me. My deepest gratitude also goes to Corinne Valette and all at DMC for their confidence from the beginning, their kindness, and their gorgeous colorful threads!

A thousand thanks to my grandmother for her indispensable help in tailoring—I'd be lost without it! A special thanks to my mother for teaching me these skills and more! And thanks to my father for drinks and snacks to lift my spirits. I love you all.

A huge thank-you to Pascale for his Friday coffees, his confidence, and his enthusiasm. All my admiration to Hiroko and Vanya for their wonderful work—thank you both—and to Denis for his help! Thank you, Dominique, for your patience. You get stuck with the tough questions and leave me speechless—I wouldn't like to take your place!

Finally, lots of love to Mona, Zélie and Mia. Their little faces light up my life.

This book is dedicated to dear Nathalie, creator of Lili Points, with whom I talked so much about this project. And to Caroline.

contents

preface

For those who love chic, modern embroidery and cross-stitch, this book is a true treasure trove of inspiration and motifs. It features only the sweetest, most heart-melting designs, from romantic hearts to cuddly teddy bears, gentle angels and fanciful fairies to alphabets that spell out tender messages.

If you've never tried embroidery or cross-stitch before (or if you have some experience but need a refresher), the techniques section, Stitching Essentials, is a great place to start. You'll learn how to work with fabric and floss, transfer motifs, and create the basic stitches that are the foundation for all of the motifs in this book.

The more than 900 motifs presented here can be applied to virtually anything, if it's made of fabric: clothing and accessories, children's garments, home accessories, and even hand-stitched cozies for your electronics. More than 70 project ideas using these motifs are provided, but the possibilities are limited only by your own imagination.

There are also instructions for sewing simple projects that you can embellish with your embroidery and cross-stitch. Of course, all of these motifs can be applied to any pre-made garments and linens for an easy, updated look.

Whether you've been stitching for years or you're picking up a needle and thread for the first time, these whimsical designs are sure to inspire. Stitching never looked so sweet!

stitching
essentials

before you begin

Before you start, make sure your fabric is well prepared so it won't fray as you're stitching it. You can either hem the edges with a large basting stitch, or simply apply strips of fusible web around the fabric's perimeter. Keep in mind that the piece of fabric should always be larger than the pattern to be stitched.

working with fabric

Fold your fabric in four to find its center point. Make large basting stitches along both the horizontal and vertical folds to serve as guidelines as you stitch. Align the center point of your motif with the point where the two lines of stitching intersect. Remove these guidelines once you've finished embroidering your motif.

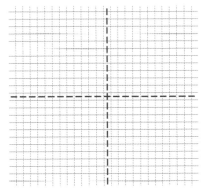

To help your stitches stay even, use an embroidery hoop. Gently stretch your fabric on the hoop, making sure to reposition it frequently—and to remove it at the end of each stitching session—to avoid damaging the fabric's weave.

embroidery floss

Two to three strands of six-strand cotton floss were used to stitch all of the projects shown in this book. Whenever you start a project, you'll find it helpful to make a sampler of stitches on the fabric you're planning to use to determine how many strands of floss you'll need.

As a general rule, lower-count Aidas—a type of counted thread fabric that's traditionally used for cross-stitch projects—require more strands, while higher-count Aidas and linens need fewer. (Cross-stitch can also be worked on other types of fabric when waste canvas is used; see page 21 for more information.) For example, most projects stitched on 14-count Aida require three strands of floss, while those stitched on 28-count linen, which has a much tighter weave, would probably need just two strands, and even one might look fine. Note that a fabric's thread count will also affect the size of your image: lower thread counts will yield larger motifs, while higher thread counts will produce smaller ones.

transferring motifs

To transfer motifs to your fabric, use carbon transfer paper, which is specially made for embroidery and is available in several colors. Choose the one that works best with your fabric. For example, white transfer paper is best for dark fabrics, while blue or red work best on lighter ones.

Start by photocopying the motif, which you can enlarge or reduce to get it to just the right size. Trace the photocopied motif on a sheet of tracing paper, following its outline and making sure to include all its details. Iron your fabric carefully before spreading it out on a flat surface, such as an ironing board or clean work table.

Place the transfer paper between the fabric and the tracing paper, making sure to put the colored side of the transfer paper face down. Keep the papers in place by pinning them to the fabric. With a hard pencil or a pen, carefully trace the motif, pressing down so that the entire image transfers properly. Once you've finished, separate the papers and fabric carefully to avoid smudging the fabric.

starting and ending off

This method of starting and ending off avoids having to tie knots on the back of your piece. To begin, take about a yard of floss, using as many strands as you need for your project. Fold it in two, then thread the needle. Bring the needle up through the fabric, leaving the loop created by the folded floss at the back. Bring the needle back down to start your first stitch, passing it through the loop, then pull gently to lock in the thread. Once you're done stitching, slip your thread under your last three or four stitches.

Before you begin, review the steps on the following pages. Even experienced stitchers are sure to find tips and hints to make their work easier.

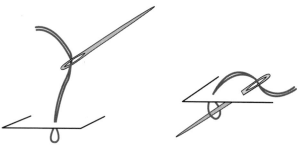

basic stitches

To embroider the motifs in this book, you'll need to learn just six easy stitches. For cross-stitch you can use one of two techniques; most of the embroidery motifs use stem stitch, except for some of the smaller details, which are noted in each motif.

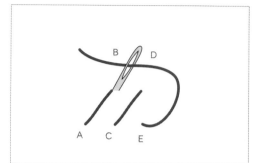

CROSS-STITCH METHOD 1

This method is especially useful for making rows of stitches. Come up through the fabric at point A, then go back down at point B, up at C, down at D. Come back up at E and, working in the opposite direction, go down at B to form an X.

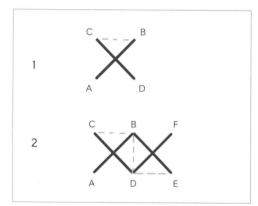

CROSS-STITCH METHOD 2

This method can be used to make either rows of cross-stitches or to make individual stitches.

1. Come up at point A, go down at B, come back up at C, then down at D to form the first cross-stitch.

2. Come back up at B, go down at E, come up at D, then go down at F to form the second cross-stitch.

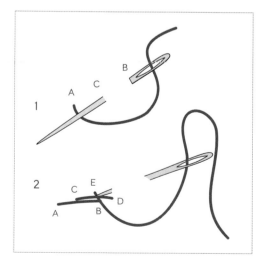

STEM STITCH

Stem stitches create a continuous yet slightly staggered line.

1. Bring the needle up at point A, then into B and up at C (midway between A and B). Note that the thread should loop *under* the needle.

2. Go down at point D and come back up at B. Note that the thread should loop *above* the needle. To make the next stitch, go down at D and come back up at E, above the previous stitch and midway along its length.

BACKSTITCH

Backstitching creates a continuous line of even stitches. Bring the needle up at point A, down at B (the end of the previous stitch) and back up at C. To make the next stitch, bring the needle down at point A, then up at point C, and continue.

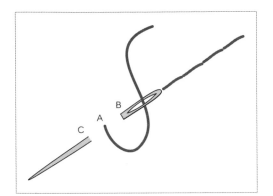

STRAIGHT STITCH

The straight stitch is the simplest of all stitches. Bring the needle up at point A, down at B, then back up at C. Make sure not to make the stitches too long. If needed, straight stitches can be made right next to each other to fill areas with solid color.

FRENCH KNOT

French knots can be used to make eyes, speckles, spots, and other small details.

1. Bring the needle up at point A. Hold the thread taut and wrap it around the needle twice.

2. Without letting go of the thread, go back down into A, slipping the needle through the wraps to form a knot.

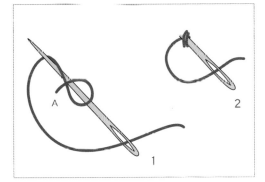

LAZY DAISY/CHAIN STITCH

A lazy daisy, or detached chain stitch, can be worked singly; one after the other, in a continuous length; or arranged in a circle to create a flower.

1. Bring the needle up at point A. Form a loop, then go back in through A and down at B so that the needle passes over the loop.

2. Finish by going back down into the fabric at C (right below B) to make a tiny stitch to keep the loop in place.

stitching with color

We selected a variety of colors both for the fabrics we used to make the projects and for the flosses we used to stitch the motifs. Depending on the theme of the project and the motif we chose to embellish it, we worked with single colors; with tints, tones, and shades of a single color; and with a wide range of colors.

The color palettes beneath each cross-stitch motif indicate numbers corresponding to the color of DMC-brand floss. If you are using another brand of embroidery floss, you can convert these numbers using the chart on page 238 to find similar shades.

Although the motifs are printed in the colors that we used for each project, feel free to use your imagination and creativity to change a palette completely, or to incorporate other colors where only one is shown.

projects for stitching

This section is an overview of how to work with some purchased items you can customize with embroidery or cross-stitch, as well as those you can easily make yourself if you're a sewer.

GARMENTS

Stitching garments—T-shirts, onesies, blouses, jackets—with embroidery and cross-stitch motifs is an easy and fun way to personalize them. See pages 45, 88, 165, and 172 for some project ideas. Always pre-wash garments to avoid shrinkage and keep colors from running, dry them as directed on the label, and press them to straighten the fabric grain.

If you're stitching an embroidery motif, you only need to transfer it to your garment. If you've chosen a cross-stitch motif and the garment—or any project—is made with a tightly woven fabric that doesn't have a visible counted-thread weave, you'll need to use waste canvas as a foundation grid to guide your stitching. Waste canvas (sometimes called blue line canvas) is a special, disposable canvas that's sold at craft and fabric stores. Before you purchase waste canvas, consider which size you want to use for your motif. As with counted-thread fabrics, the waste canvas's thread count will have an effect on the size and look of your motif.

Cut a piece of waste canvas that's large enough to accommodate your motif, at least an inch larger all around; repeat for the accompanying interfacing, which goes on the inside of the garment. Fold the cut pieces of the waste canvas and the interfacing into quarters to locate their center points and position the waste canvas over the area you want to stitch. Insert the interfacing on the inside of the garment directly beneath the waste canvas, pin them in place, then baste them onto the garment. Always start a cross-stitch motif at its center point to hold the waste canvas and interfacing in place.

Once you've finished stitching, trim the interfacing on the inside of the garment, then remove the waste canvas's threads by dampening them with water, then pulling them out with your fingers or a tweezer.

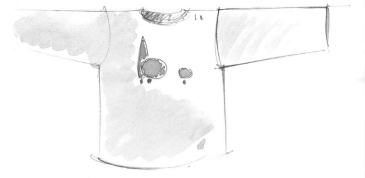

PILLOWS AND CUSHION COVERS

You can stitch a motif on a purchased pillow cover, or you can easily make a simple envelope-style pillow cover yourself.

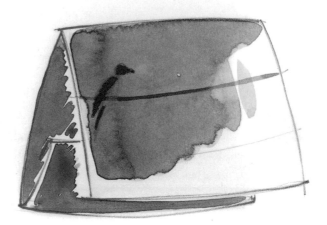

Start by measuring the pillow. Cut a piece of fabric the same width as the pillow and long enough that will fit around the pillow plus ½ to 4 inches/1.25 to 10cm for a flap. (The flap could be either on the front or the back of the pillow.) Since your pillow cover may need to be washed at some point, we recommend that you wash and press the fabric before stitching it.

Stitch your motifs on the fabric, making sure beforehand that they'll be positioned correctly when the finished cover is placed on the pillow.

une étoi le estnée

Hem the fabric by folding each edge under ¼ inch/0.6cm, pressing with an iron, then stitching into place. Fold the cover into correct shape. With wrong sides together stitch the sides closed, then turn it right side out and attach a ribbon or button closure.

TABLECLOTHS AND NAPKINS

Stitching is a great way to make a plain purchased tablecloth and napkins into treasured family heirlooms. See pages 38 and 84 for some examples. Be sure to wash and press these items before you stitch them, as they'll undoubtedly need to be washed after you and your guests use them.

To determine where you want to stitch your napkins, you'll need to fold one in the style you prefer. For a tablecloth, the traditional place for a stitch motif is its center, but you could also spread it out on your table to see if another placement would work better.

STORAGE BOX LINERS

Dressing up a small box with a stitched linen-and-cotton liner is a great way to create a beautiful storage solution. The fabric-lined baby organizer on page 168 is a great gift idea.

Adapt the design shown below to the size of your box. For our liner, we used striped cotton (for the bottom of the liner) and white linen (for the top, or exposed side), cutting pattern pieces for each side twice in the linen and twice in the cotton. (Be sure to wash and press the fabric before cutting and stitching it.) Cut 2¾ yards/2.4m of ribbon into eight equal lengths.

Embroider the motifs on the linen. Sew together each of the four sides and bottom as shown in the drawing below, then press the seams with an iron. Repeat for the striped cotton.

Place the assembled pieces right sides together and slip the cut pieces of ribbon between the two layers as shown. Leaving one side open, sew the pieces together ½ inch/1cm from the edge so that one end of each ribbon is sewn into the seam.

Turn the liner right side out, make a ½ inch/1cm hem on each side of the opening and hand-sew it closed. Place the liner in the box and tie the ribbons.

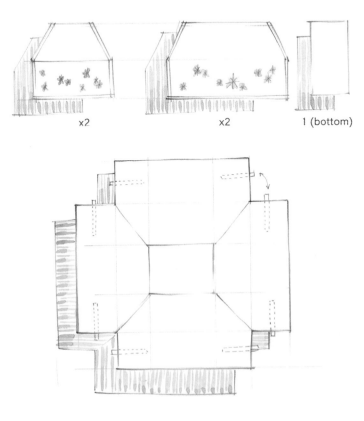

x2   x2   1 (bottom)

BACKPACK

This simple backpack can be made from any stitchable fabric, from casual to dressy. See page 157 for an example, which we made from linen and lined with printed cotton.

Stitch the pattern in the center of one half of a piece of linen measuring 14 x 32 inches/35 x 80cm. Fold the linen right sides together and slip two pieces of ribbon each measuring 1¼ yards/2.25m between the two sides of the bag as shown so that their ends are sandwiched in the bottom side seams. Sew the sides together, leaving an opening of ¾ inch to 2 inches/1.5 to 5cm from the top of each side. Make a double flap

on the back, ½ inch and 1 inch/1cm and 3cm, then press.

Fold a piece of cotton lining measuring 14 x 27 inches/35 x 68cm in half, wrong sides together, and sew the sides. Make a ½ inch/1cm hem at the top and press. Slide the linen bag into the cotton lining, then sew the two together with an overlap hem of ¼ inch/0.5 cm. Turn the bag right side in, then string 1 yard/1m of ribbon all the way through the overlap; repeat with a second 1 yard/1m of ribbon, working it through the overlap in the other direction.

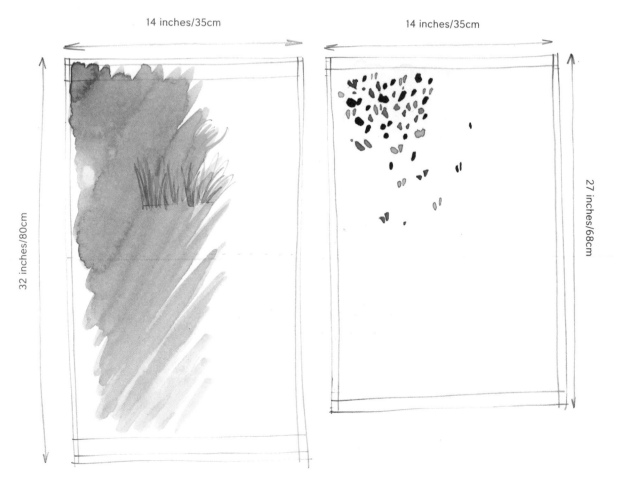

14 inches/35cm

14 inches/35cm

32 inches/80cm

27 inches/68cm

BIB

This is such an easy gift to stitch and sew, you can make several at a time. To make the example shown on page 210, we used 16-count linen and two different cotton prints (one for the front panel and one for the back of the bib) with a waffle-weave fabric in between them as a light batting. We used 11½ x 12¼ inches/29 x 31cm of each fabric and 2 yards/1.8m of bias tape to finish the edges. Bibs are made for messes, so be sure to wash and press your fabrics before cutting and stitching them.

Use the large bib template on page 236 to cut its shape from the linen, the cotton print for the back, and the waffle-weave fabric. Use the area on the template marked by a dotted line to cut the cotton print panel for the front.

Stitch your motif on the linen, then sew the cotton print panel to it. Create the layers for the bib "sandwich" by starting with the cotton for the back, wrong side up, then the waffle-weave fabric, and finally the stitch linen right side up. Pin the bias tape around the edge of the bib. Sew around the edges of the whole bib first, and then sew the neckline.

BABY COVERLET

This little blanket is yet another simple-to-make, simply lovely baby gift. See our example on page 174, which we made with 30¼ x 50 inches/72 x 127cm of 16-count linen and inches 27½ inches/70cm of lace trim. Wash and press the fabrics before stitching.

Stitch the motif on the linen about 3 inches/7cm from one end and 12 inches/30cm from one side edge of the fabric. Machine-sew a double hem of ¼ inch and ½ inch/0.5 and 1.5cm on the sides; a double hem of ½ inch and 1¼ inch/1 and 3cm on the bottom; and a double hem of ½ inch and ¾ inch/1 and 2cm at the top. By hand, make another 1¼ inch/3cm hem at the top, then sew on the lace.

1¾ inches/4cm

12 inches/30cm

½ inch + ¾ inch/1 + 2cm

47 inches/120cm

½ inch + 1¼ inches/1 + 3cm

28¾ inches/73cm

¼ inch + ½ inch/0.5 + 1.5cm

¼ inch + ½ inch/0.5 + 1.5cm

CHANGING PAD

This project requires just a little more time and
effort to make than the coverlet on page 27. We
made our changing pad, shown on page 90, with
beautiful 16-count linen: two 25- x 35-inch/64
x 89cm pieces for the pad and two 10¼- x
18-inch/26 x 46cm pieces for the little pillow.
The pad will need to be washable, so be sure to
wash and press your fabrics prior to cutting and
stitching them.

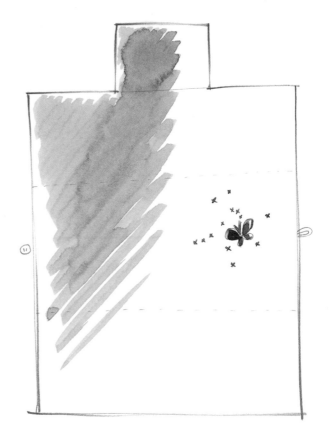

To give both the pad and the pillow extra
softness, we used fluffy cotton batting: a 24½- x
34¼-inch/62 x 87cm piece for the pad and a 9½-
x 8¼-inch/24 x 21cm piece for the pillow. The
bias-tape-and-button closure makes the pad easy
to roll up and tote in a diaper bag.

Stitch motifs as desired on the large fabric pieces.
Sew 4 inches/10cm of bias tape along its length
so that it won't open, then fold it in half and stitch the very ends of the tape to the edge of the wrong
side of the back piece, at the center of its length. Sew a large button to the right side of the back piece
opposite the bias tape loop.

Place the two large pieces of linen together, right sides facing. Stitch all around ½ inch/1cm from the
edge, leaving a wide opening on the top end. Press the seams open and turn the pad right side out, then
slip in the batting. Set aside.

To make the little pillow, stitch the motifs on the right side of one end of the linen, then fold the fabric
right sides together and sew the sides ½ inch/1cm from the edge. Press the seams open, turn the pillow
right side out, and slip the batting inside.

Fold in the edges of the opening on the pad ½ inch/1cm, slip in ¾ inch/2cm of the unfinished pillow
edge, and sew the opening of the pad closed ½ inch/1cm from the edge.

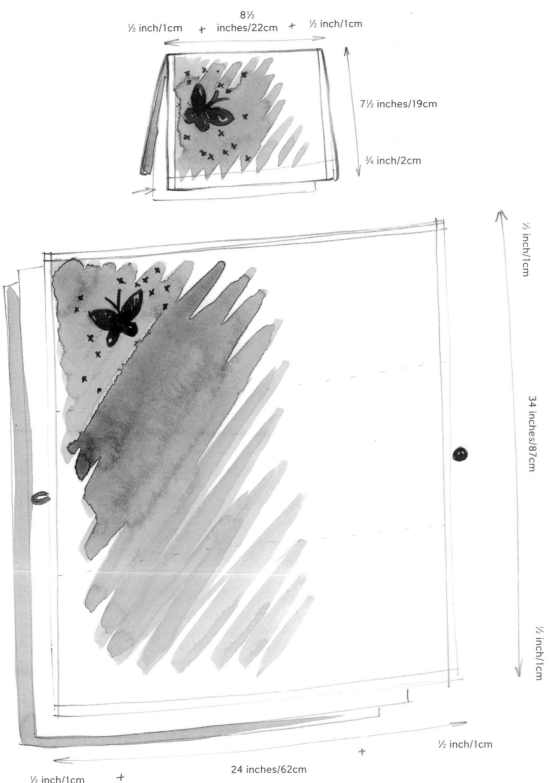

8½ inches/22cm

½ inch/1cm + + ½ inch/1cm

7½ inches/19cm

¾ inch/2cm

½ inch/1cm

34 inches/87cm

½ inch/1cm

½ inch/1cm

24 inches/62cm

½ inch/1cm +

+

CRIB VEIL

This charming crib veil is perfect for any tiny princess. We used 4¼ yards/4m of soft pink tulle to make the example on page 89. The advantages of using tulle for this project is that you don't have to hem it—though you do need to cut it straight—and you don't need waste canvas to stitch it because the netting itself serves as the stitch grid.

Stitch the motifs as desired. You can be creative and place them wherever you'd like, but be sure to keep them close to the edges and away from the center of the fabric or they'll get caught in the pleats or gathered at the top.

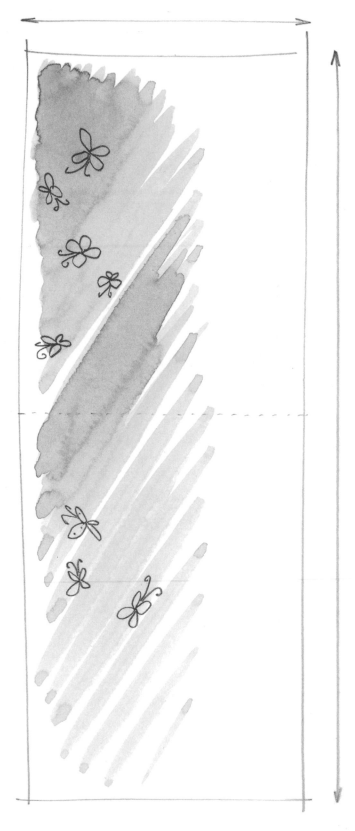

4¼ yards/4m

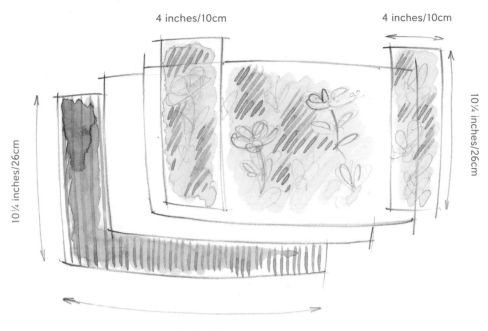

4 inches/10cm

4 inches/10cm

10¼ inches/26cm

10¼ inches/26cm

13½ inches/34cm

KEEPSAKE FOLDER

A handmade folder can be used to keep photos, cards, letters, and other special documents. Ours (see page 156) is made with two cotton prints—we used a stripe for the exterior and a green print for the inside—with thin cotton batting in between. You'll need 10¼ x 13½ inches/26 x 34cm of each, plus two ¾ x 7¾ x 10¼-inch/2 x 20 x 26cm pieces of the inside print for the folder flaps and 1¾ yards/1.7m of bias tape in a contrasting color to finish the edges and make a tie closure.

Stitch the motif on the exterior fabric as desired. Lay the stitched fabric right side down, cover it with the batting, then place the inside fabric right side up. Fold the fabric pieces for the flaps in half lengthwise, wrong sides together, and place them at the edges of the inside fabric.

Cut two 6-inch/15cm lengths of bias tape; set aside. Pin the remaining bias tape around the edges of the sandwich. Before sewing the sandwich together ¼ inch/1cm from the edge, insert each of the 6-inch/15cm lengths of bias tape underneath the edging to make the closure.

hearts

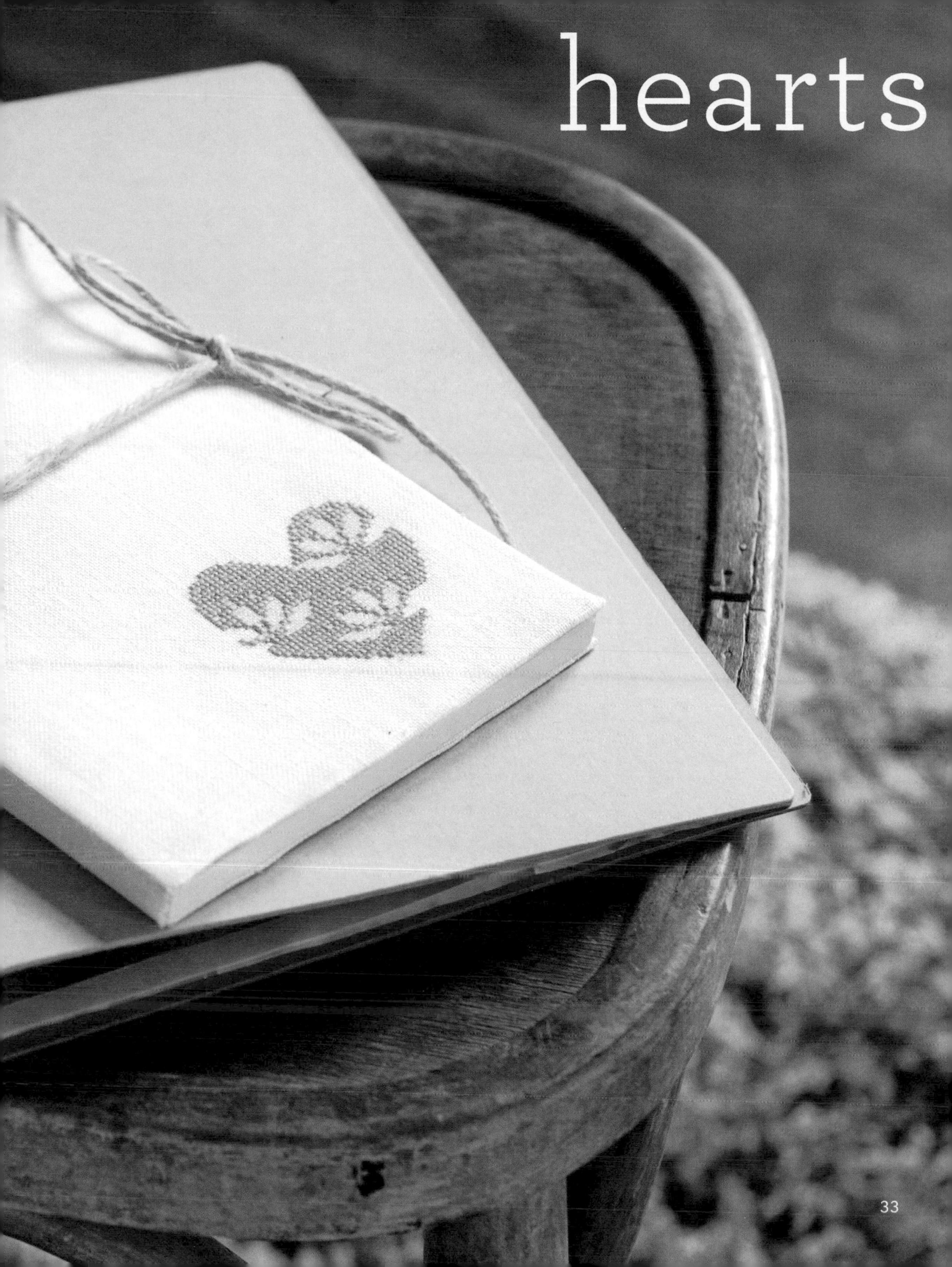

1. Sewn with Love Thread Box

See motifs on pages 48–49

2· Lacy Heart Needle Case

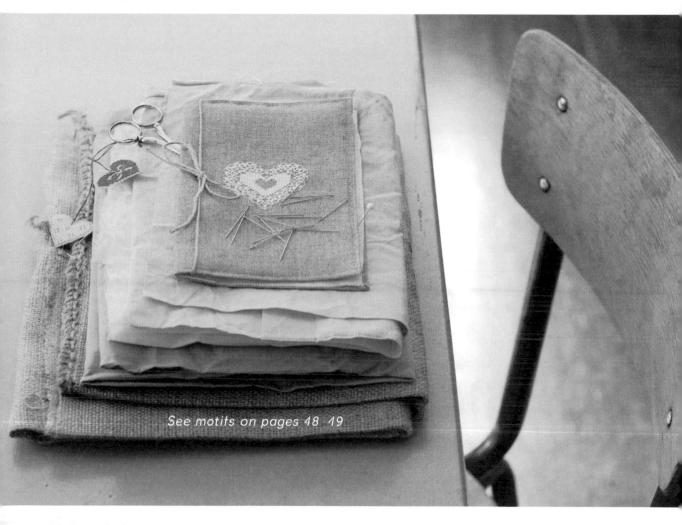

See motifs on pages 48–49

3· Cookie Love Apron

See motifs on pages 50–51

4. Heart of the Home Shade

See motifs on pages 52–53

5. Love Is a Rose Napkin

See motifs on pages 54–55

6. Heirloom Tablecloth

See motifs on pages 56–58

7. Love Note Keeper

See motifs on pages 60–61

(PAPIERS)

8. Leaves Me Speechless Pillow

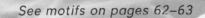

See motifs on pages 62–63

LOVE FOR EVER

(••)

••••

9. Love Forever Keepsake

See motifs on pages 64–65

louise et gabriel

See motifs on pages 64–65

11. Lovestruck Blouse

See motifs on page 66

12. Sweet Tees

See motifs on page 67

See motifs on pages 68–69

14. Heart of Hearts Sampler

See motifs on pages 70–71

heart motifs

1 & 2. Lacy Hearts

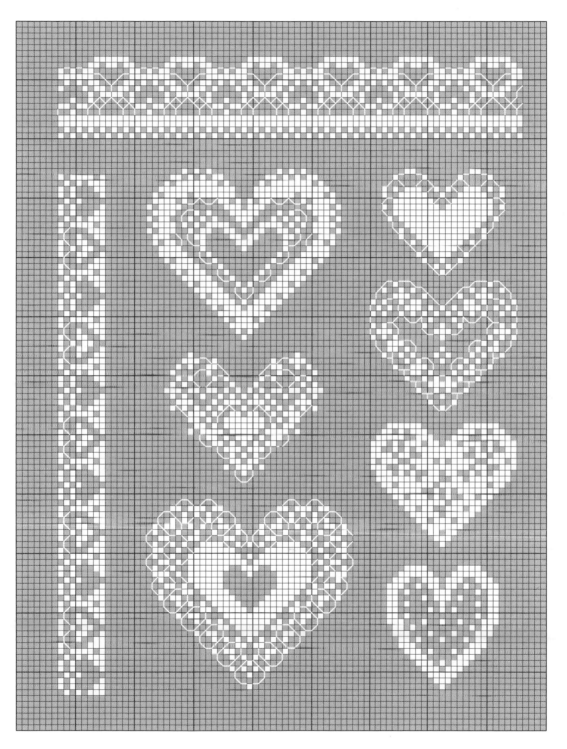

See projects on pages 34 and 35

3· Sweets for the Sweet

stem stitch
2 strands

backstitch
3 strands

backstitch
2 strands

I LOVE

backstitch
2 strands

stem stitch
2 strands

straight stitch
1 stem

backstitch
2 strands

backstitch
2 strands

stem stitch
2 strands

straight stitch
1 strand

straight stitch
1 strand

stem stitch
2 strands

backstitch
2 strands

stem stitch
2 strands

stem stitch
2 strands

straight stitch
1 strand

backstitch
2 strands

French knot
1 strand

backstitch
2 strands

backstitch
2 strands

backstitch
2 strands

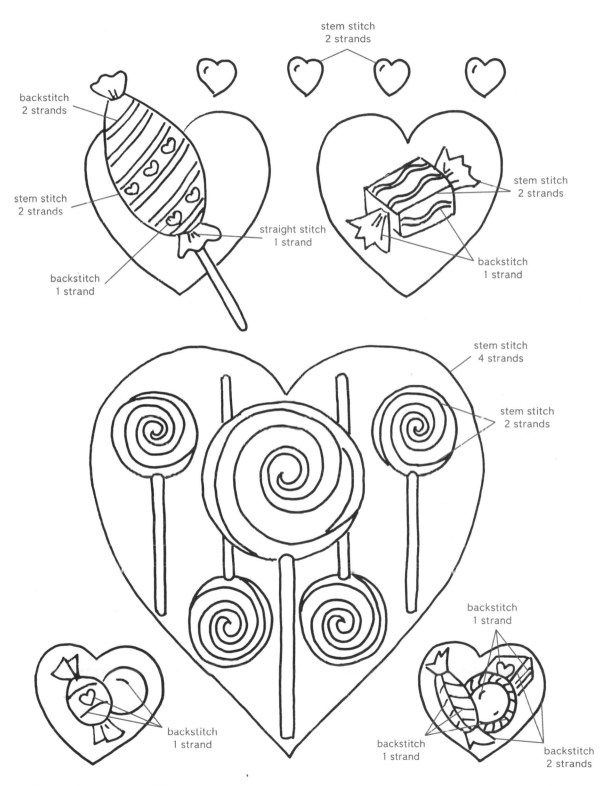

stem stitch
2 strands

backstitch
2 strands

stem stitch
2 strands

stem stitch
2 strands

straight stitch
1 strand

backstitch
1 strand

backstitch
1 strand

stem stitch
4 strands

stem stitch
2 strands

backstitch
1 strand

backstitch
1 strand

backstitch
1 strand

backstitch
1 strand

backstitch
2 strands

See project on page 36

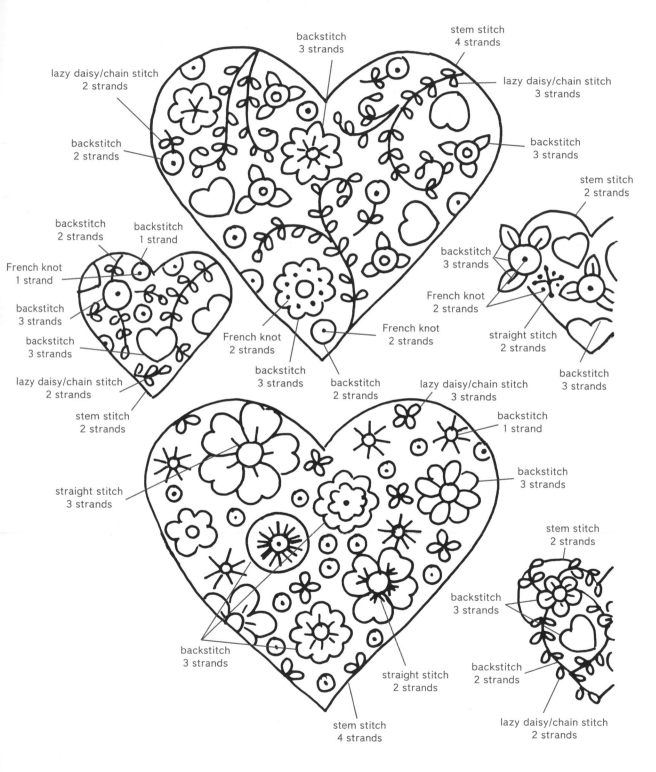

lazy daisy/chain stitch
2 strands

backstitch
3 strands

stem stitch
4 strands

lazy daisy/chain stitch
3 strands

backstitch
2 strands

backstitch
3 strands

stem stitch
2 strands

backstitch
2 strands

backstitch
1 strand

French knot
1 strand

backstitch
3 strands

French knot
2 strands

backstitch
3 strands

backstitch
3 strands

French knot
2 strands

straight stitch
2 strands

lazy daisy/chain stitch
2 strands

backstitch
3 strands

stem stitch
2 strands

French knot
2 strands

backstitch
3 strands

backstitch
2 strands

lazy daisy/chain stitch
3 strands

backstitch
1 strand

backstitch
3 strands

straight stitch
3 strands

stem stitch
2 strands

backstitch
3 strands

backstitch
3 strands

straight stitch
2 strands

backstitch
2 strands

stem stitch
4 strands

lazy daisy/chain stitch
2 strands

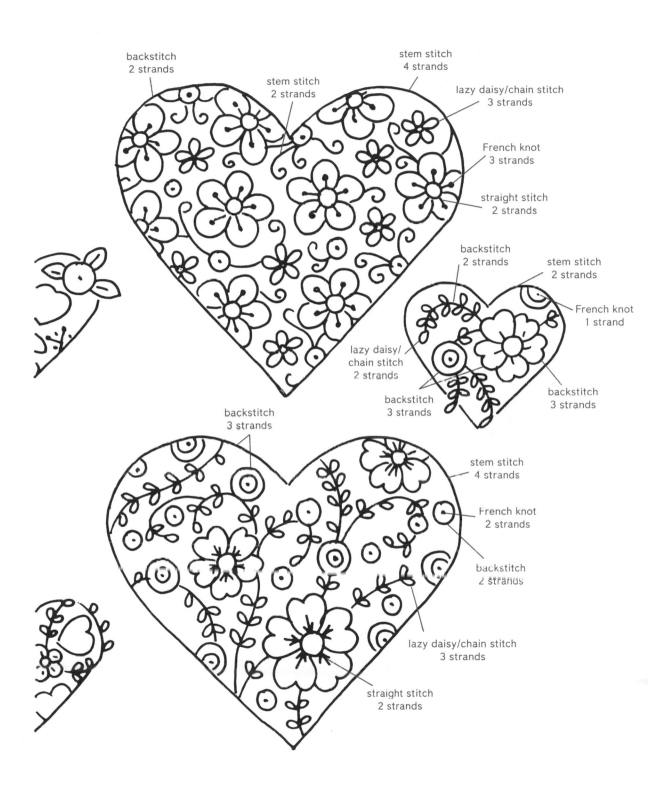

backstitch
2 strands

stem stitch
2 strands

stem stitch
4 strands

lazy daisy/chain stitch
3 strands

French knot
3 strands

straight stitch
2 strands

backstitch
2 strands

stem stitch
2 strands

French knot
1 strand

lazy daisy/
chain stitch
2 strands

backstitch
3 strands

backstitch
3 strands

backstitch
3 strands

stem stitch
4 strands

French knot
2 strands

backstitch
2 strands

lazy daisy/chain stitch
3 strands

straight stitch
2 strands

See project on page 37

53

5. Rose Is a Rose

lazy daisy/chain stitch
2 strands

lazy daisy/chain stitch
2 strands

backstitch
3 strand

backstitch
3 strands

lazy daisy/chain stitch
3 strands

backstitch
3 strands

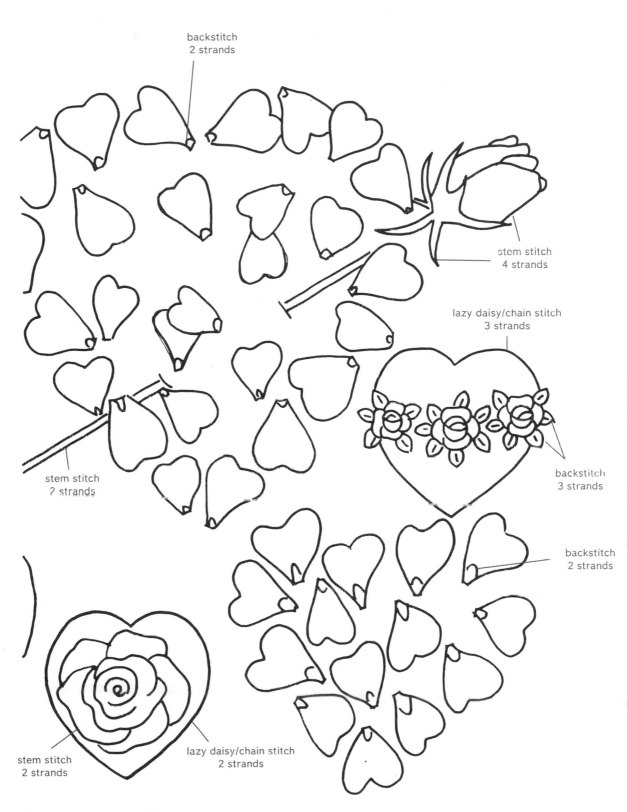

backstitch
2 strands

stem stitch
4 strands

lazy daisy/chain stitch
3 strands

backstitch
3 strands

stem stitch
2 strands

backstitch
2 strands

stem stitch
2 strands

lazy daisy/chain stitch
2 strands

See project on page 38

6. Heirloom Heart

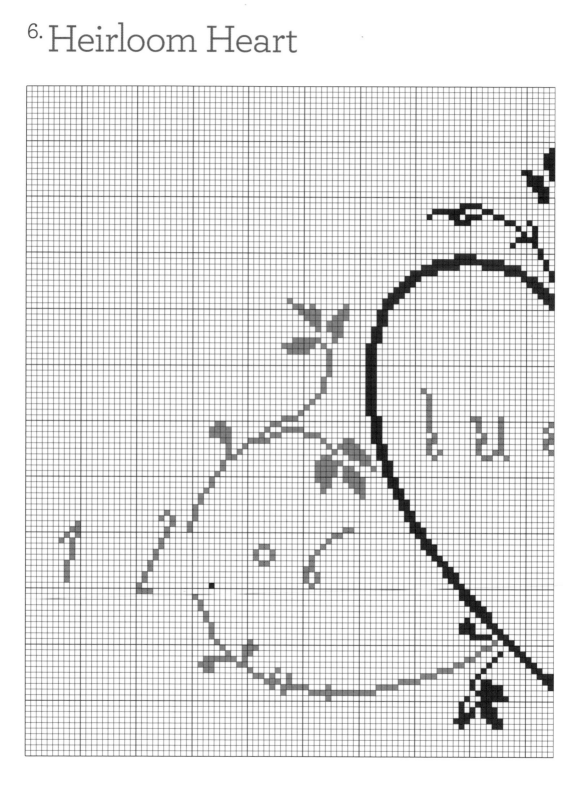

See project on page 39

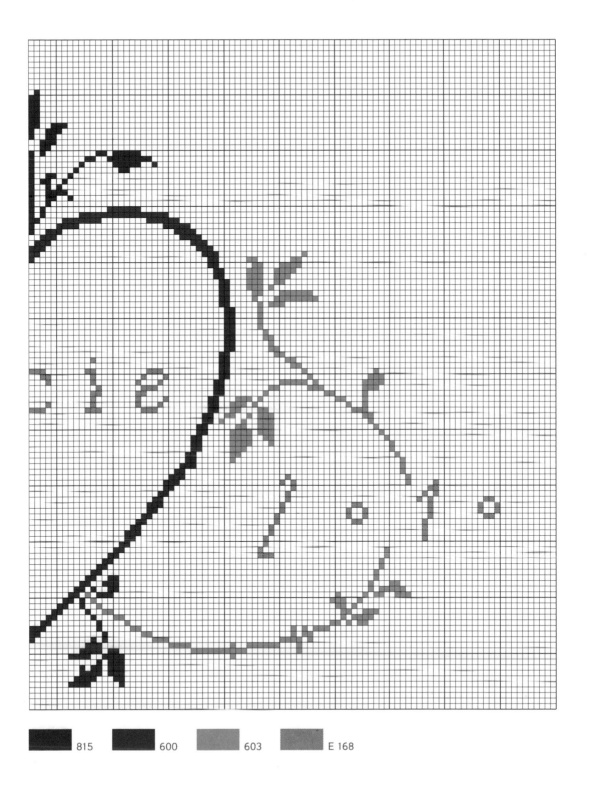

815   600   603   E 168

6. Heirloom Heart

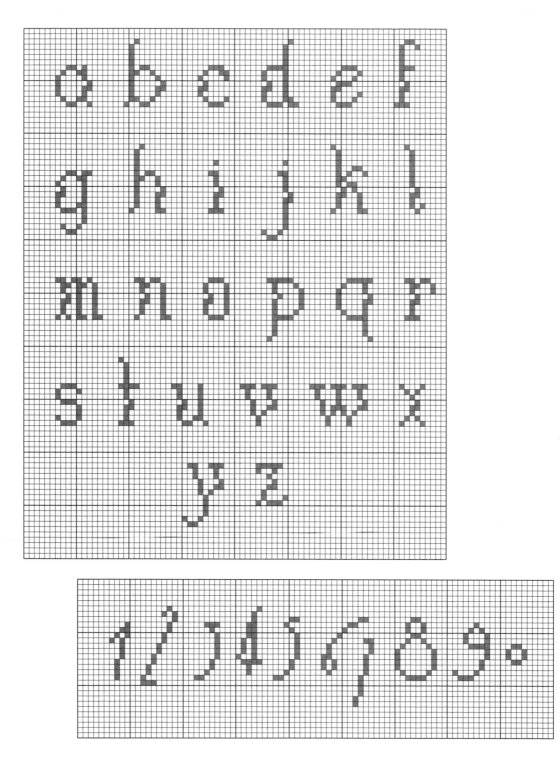

See project on page 39

Heart Beats

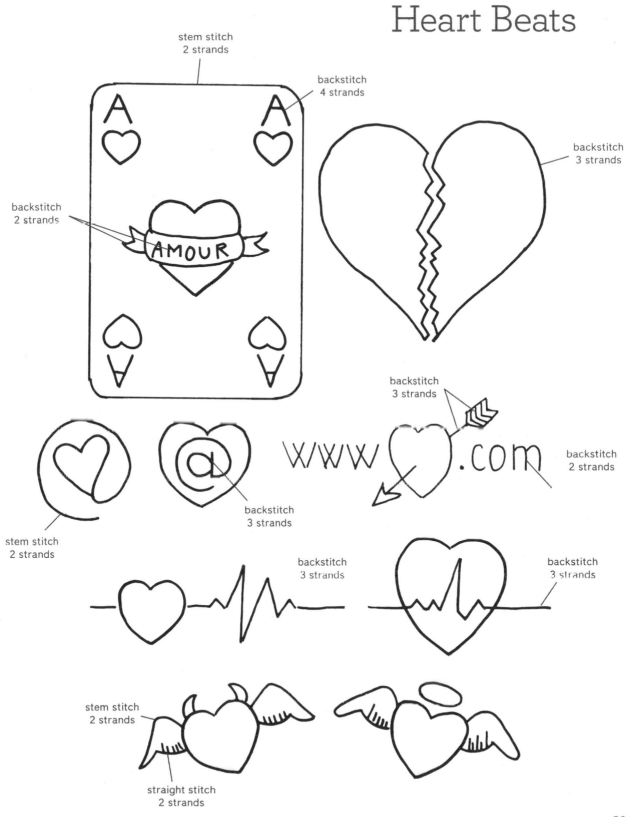

stem stitch
2 strands

backstitch
4 strands

backstitch
3 strands

backstitch
2 strands

A

A

AMOUR

backstitch
3 strands

www. .com

backstitch
2 strands

stem stitch
2 strands

backstitch
3 strands

backstitch
3 strands

backstitch
3 strands

stem stitch
2 strands

straight stitch
2 strands

7. Messages of Love

See project on page 40

See project on page 41

9 & 10. Just Married

backstitch
4 strands

lazy daisy/
chain stitch
2 strands

backstitch
1 strand

backstitch
3 strands

French knot
3 strands

backstitch
4 strands

ELSA ♡ GUILLAUME

backstitch
3 strands

lazy daisy/
chain stitch
3 strands

stem stitch
2 strands

backstitch
3 strands

POUR ♡ toujours

lazy daisy/
chain stitch
3 strands

stem stitch
2 strands

stem stitch
4 strands

overlapping
stem stitches
2 strands

stem stitch
4 strands

LO VE

French knot
2 strands

lazy daisy/
chain stitch
3 strands

Oui ♡ le 17.07.2010

backstitch
3 strands

lazy daisy/
chain stitch
3 strands

stem stitch
2 strands

stem stitch
4 strands

backstitch
4 strands

JUST MARRIED

1 2 3 4 5 6 8 9 0

64

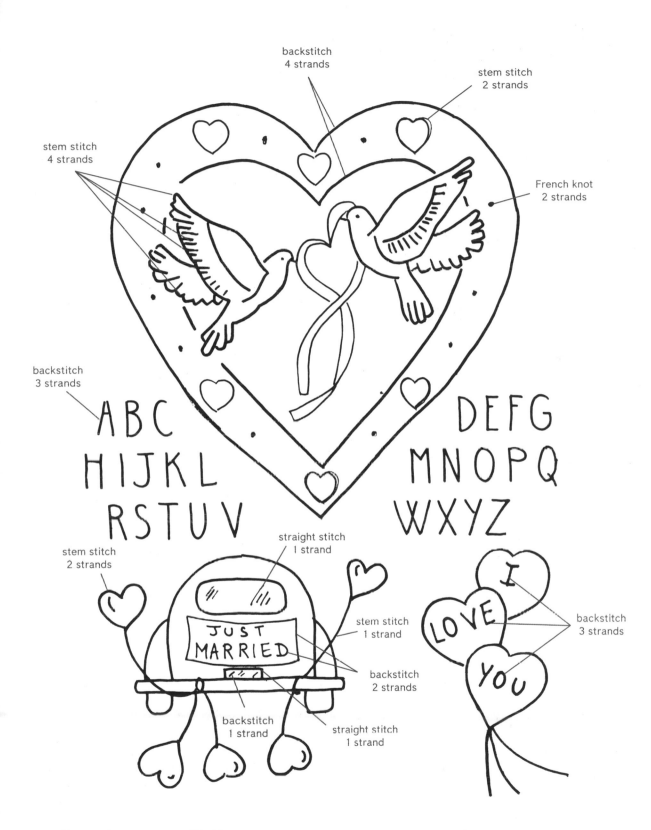

backstitch
4 strands

stem stitch
2 strands

stem stitch
4 strands

French knot
2 strands

backstitch
3 strands

ABC   DEFG
HIJKL   MNOPQ
RSTUV   WXYZ

stem stitch
2 strands

straight stitch
1 strand

stem stitch
1 strand

JUST
MARRIED

backstitch
2 strands

backstitch
1 strand

straight stitch
1 strand

I
LOVE
YOU

backstitch
3 strands

See projects on page 42–43

11. Lady Love Charms

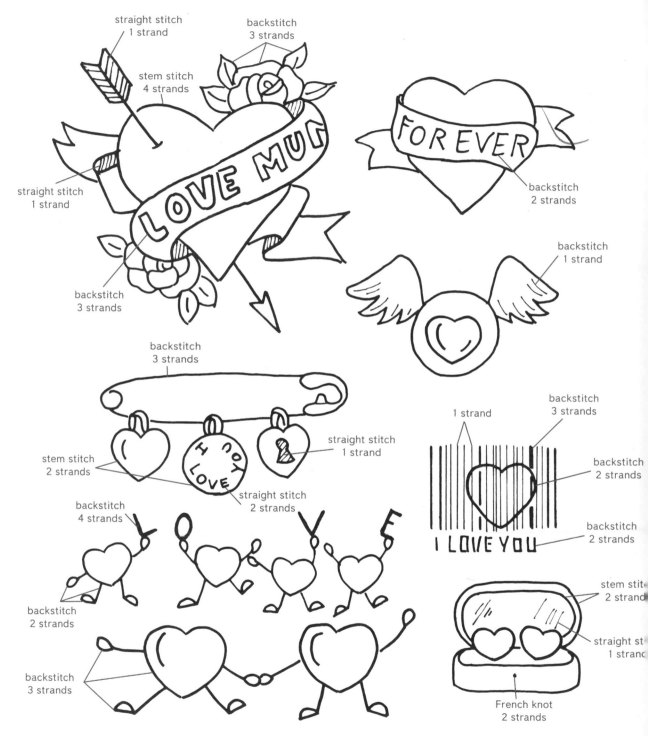

straight stitch
1 strand

backstitch
3 strands

stem stitch
4 strands

straight stitch
1 strand

backstitch
3 strands

LOVE MUM

FOR EVER

backstitch
2 strands

backstitch
1 strand

backstitch
3 strands

stem stitch
2 strands

straight stitch
1 strand

straight stitch
2 strands

1 strand

backstitch
3 strands

backstitch
2 strands

backstitch
4 strands

backstitch
2 strands

I LOVE YOU

backstitch
2 strands

stem stitch
2 strands

straight stitch
1 strand

backstitch
3 strands

French knot
2 strands

See project on page 44

12. Whimsical Strawberry & Heart

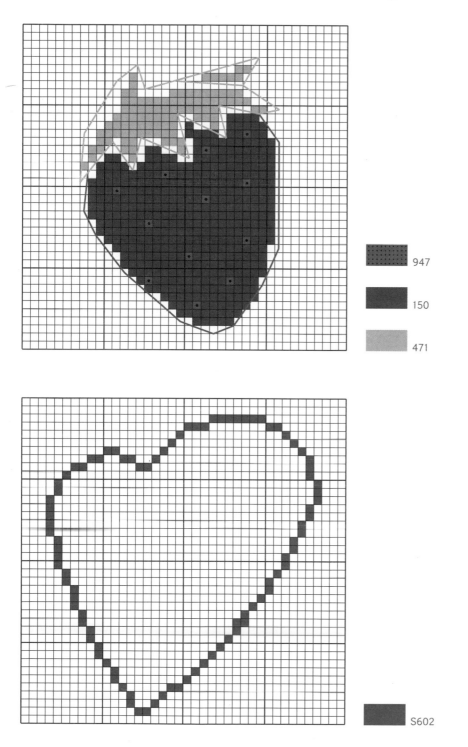

▦	947
■	150
▨	471

■	S602

See projects on page 45

13. Heart Borders

See project on page 46

A Heart of Hearts

See project on page 47

angels,
fairies &
friends

See motifs on pages 92–93

1. Blessed Dreams Pillowcases

2. Birds of Peace Lampshade

See motifs on page 94

See motifs on page 95

3· Flights of Fancy Blotter

4· Cupid's Sewing Kit

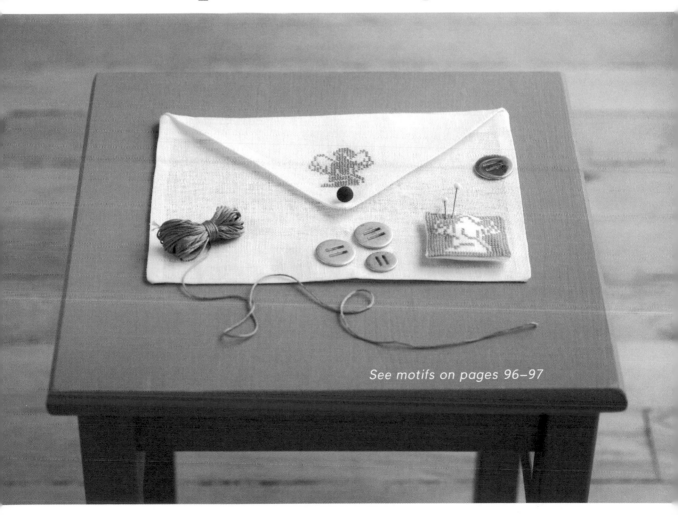

See motifs on pages 96–97

5. Fairies Tête-à-tête Toddler Top

See motifs on pages 98–99

6. Lookout Fairy Tee

See motifs on pages 98–99

7. Angel on My Pocket

See motifs on page 100

8. Special Occasion Linens Box

See motifs on page 101

See motifs on pages 102–103

9· Butterfly Bucket Cover

10. Garden Fairy Apron

See motifs on pages 104–105

11. Table Graces Tablecloth

See motifs on pages 106–107

12. Wings of Love Napkins

See motifs on pages 108–109

13. Angel Baby Bunting

See motifs on pages 110–111

14. Flutterby Onesie

See motifs on page 112

15. Garden Canopy Crib Veil

See motifs on page 112
See project instructions on page 30

See motifs on page 113

See project instructions on page 28

16. Lacewing Changing Pad

^{17.} Charming Fairy Diaper Tote

See motifs on page 103

angels, fairies
& friends motifs

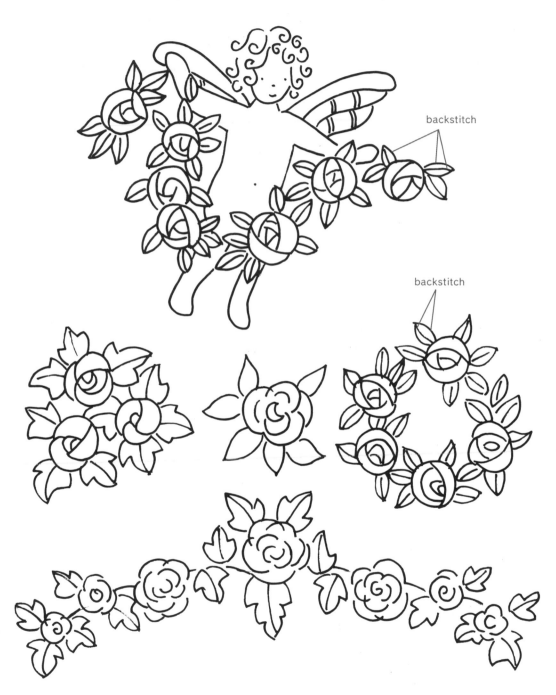

backstitch

backstitch

¹·Angels & Garlands

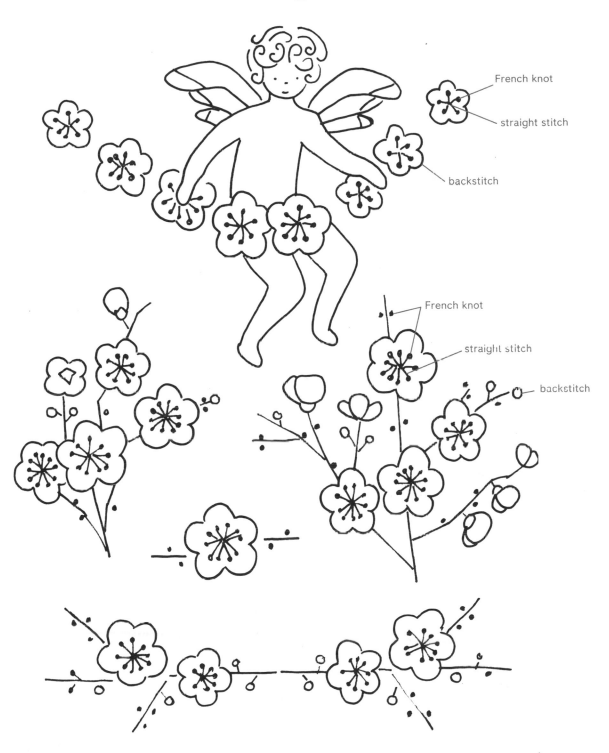

French knot

straight stitch

backstitch

French knot

straight stitch

backstitch

See project on page 74

French knot
1 strand

stem stitch
2 strands

straight stitch
2 strands

French knot
2 strands

French knot
1 strand

stem stitch
2 strands

backstitch
1 strand

French knot
3 strands

stem stitch
1 strand

French knot
2 strands

straight stitch
2 strands

stem stitch
2 strands

French knot
3 strands

backstitch
1 strand

backstitch
2 strands

stem stitch
1 strand

lazy daisy/chain stitch
1 strand

backstitch
1 strand

See project on page 75

3. Blowing in the Wind

See project on page 76

4· Light as Feathers, Free as Birds

See project on page 77

5 & 6. Busy Bee Fairies

See projects on pages 78 and 79

lazy daisy/chain stitch

French knot
1 strand

stem stitch
1 strand

stem stitch
1 strand

backstitch

See projects on pages 80 and 81

9 & 17. Fairies All Aflutter

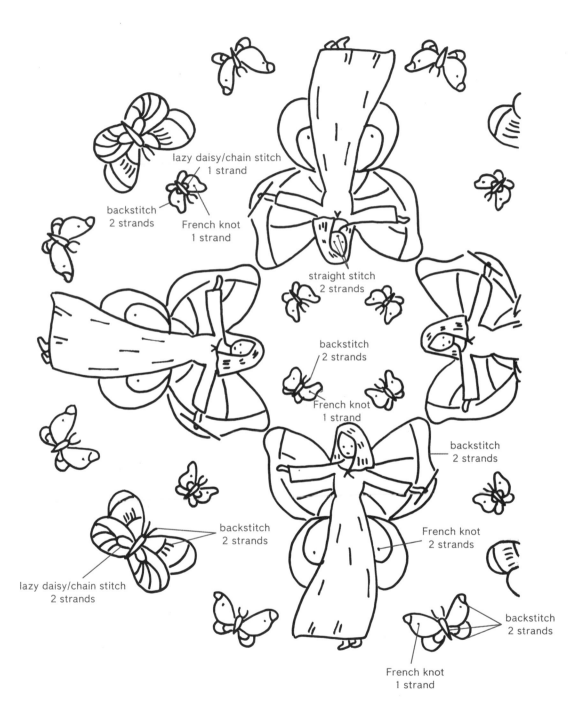

lazy daisy/chain stitch
1 strand

backstitch
2 strands

French knot
1 strand

straight stitch
2 strands

backstitch
2 strands

French knot
1 strand

backstitch
2 strands

backstitch
2 strands

French knot
2 strands

lazy daisy/chain stitch
2 strands

backstitch
2 strands

French knot
1 strand

backstitch
1 strand

lazy daisy/chain stitch
1 strand

stem stitch
2 strands

backstitch
2 strands

French knot
2 strands

backstitch
1 strand

French knot
1 strand

backstitch
2 strands

backstitch
2 strands

French knot
2 strands

backstitch
1 strand

French knot
2 strands

French knot
1 strand

See projects on pages 82 and 91

10. Fairies & Flowers

French knot
2 strands

straight stitch
2 strands

backstitch
1 strand

backstitch
1 strand

lazy daisy/chain stitch
1 strand

See project on page 83

French knot
2 strands

stem stitch
2 strands

backstitch
3 strands

French knot
1 strands

stem stitch
2 strands

stem stitch
2 strands

11. Giving Thanks

See project on page 84

12. Sweet Love

See project on page 85

¹³· A Little Angel's Wings

See project on pages 86–87

451

14 & 15. Fanciful Butterflies

See projects on pages 88 and 89

963

16. Butterflies in Cross-Stitch

600

150

154

600

See project on page 90

teddies

Merci Merci Merci

CHUT ... ON DORT

1. Yummy Honey Placemat

See motifs on pages 126–129

2. Toddling Teddies Napkins

See motifs on page 130

3. ABC—Teddy, You & Me!

See motifs on pages 132–133

4. Beary Cute Crib Toys

See motifs on pages 136–137

5. Tags for Traveling Teddies

See motifs on pages 138–139

6. Three Bears Coverlet

See motifs on pages 140–141

7. Teddy Artiste Portfolio & Brushpot

See motifs on pages 142–143

8. Bears Playtime Smock

See motifs on pages 144–145

123

9. Woodland Friends Toy Sack

See motifs on pages 146–147

124

10. Sampler with a Teddy Twist

See motifs on pages 148–149

teddies motifs

See project on page 116

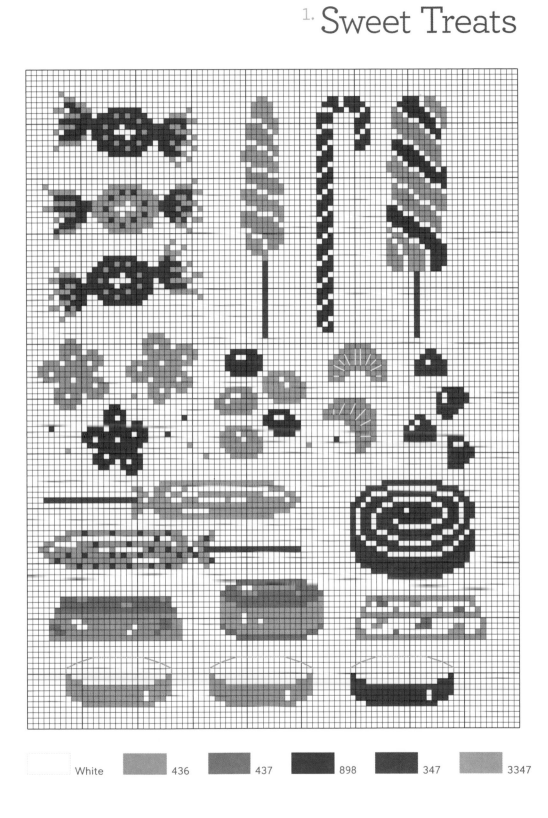

| | White | | 436 | | 437 | | 898 | | 347 | | 3347 |

Bears in Poses

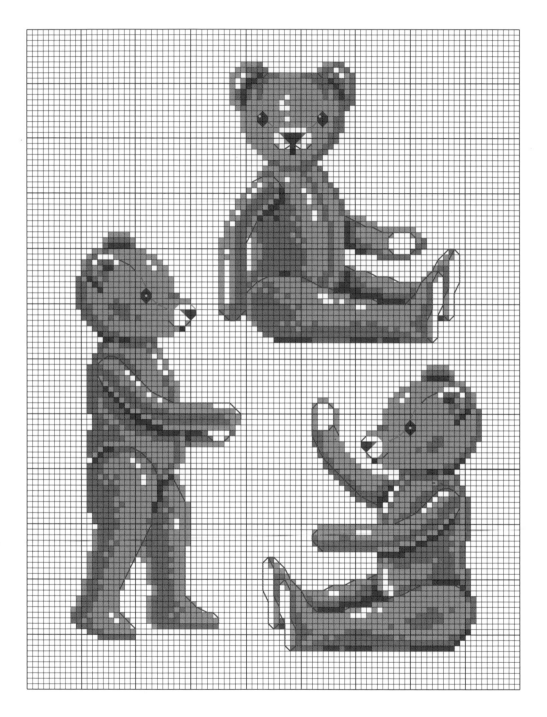

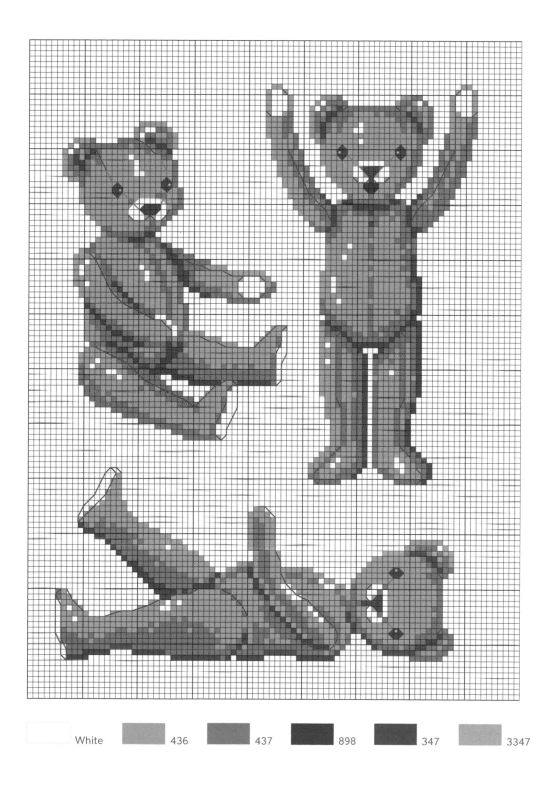

White | 436 | 437 | 898 | 347 | 3347

French knot
1 strand

fill with
stem stitch

backstitch
2 strands

straight stitch
2 strands

French knot
1 strand

See project on page 117

Backyard & Farmyard Friends

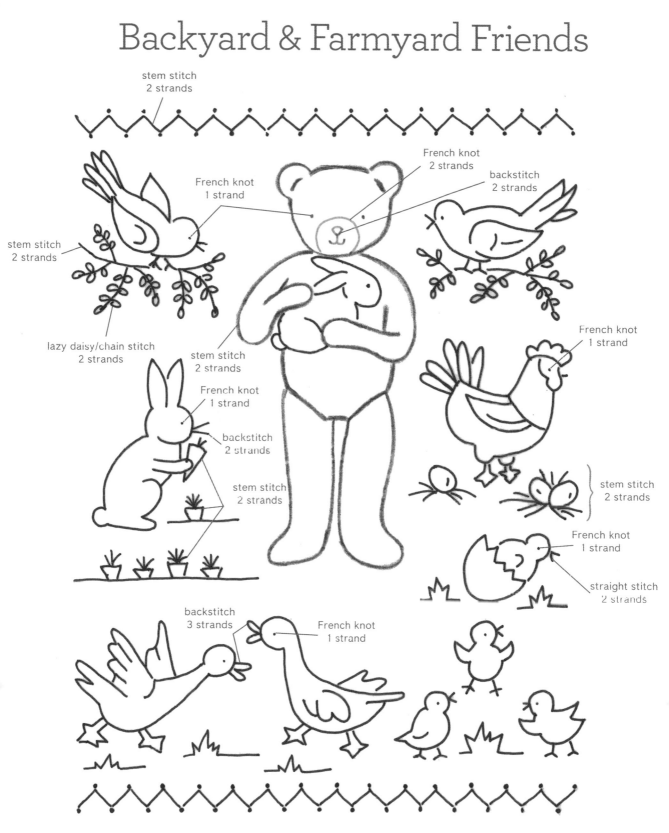

stem stitch
2 strands

French knot
2 strands

backstitch
2 strands

French knot
1 strand

stem stitch
2 strands

French knot
1 strand

lazy daisy/chain stitch
2 strands

stem stitch
2 strands

French knot
1 strand

backstitch
2 strands

stem stitch
2 strands

stem stitch
2 strands

French knot
1 strand

straight stitch
2 strands

backstitch
3 strands

French knot
1 strand

3. Alphabears

A B C D E F G H I J
K L M N O P Q R S
T U V W X Y Z

stem stitch
2 strands

a b c d e f g h i j k l m n
o p q r s t u v w x y z

backstitch
2 strands

backstitch
2 strands

straight stitch
1 strand

stem stitch
2 strands

A B C D E F G H I J
K L M N O P Q R S
T U V W X Y Z

stem stitch
2 strands

1 2 3 4 5 6 7 8 9 0

stem stitch
2 strands

backstitch
2 strands

132

stem stitch
2 strands

backstitch
2 strands

stem stitch
2 strands

backstitch
2 strands

See project on page 118

Playing Dress Up

French knot
2 strands

stem stitch
2 strands

straight stitch
2 strands

backstitch
2 strands

lazy daisy/chain stitch
3 strands

stem stitch
2 strands

French knot
2 strands

backstitch
3 strands

straight stitch
2 strands

straight stitch
2 strands

backstitch
2 strands + straight stitch

lazy daisy/chain stitch
2 strands

backstitch
3 strands

backstitch
2 strands

rows of stem stitch close together
2 strands

straight stitch
2 strands

backstitch
2 strands

for all tabs, use straight stitch
1 strand

stem stitch
2 strands

for all snowflakes,
use backstitch
1 strand

backstitch
2 strands

fill with
stem stitch
3 strands

straight stitch
1 strand

stem stitch
2 strands

backstitch
2 strands

backstitch
1 strand

stem stitch
2 strands

stem stitch
2 strands

French knot
1 strand

lazy daisy/
chain stitch
1 strand

backstitch
2 strands

backstitch
1 strand

straight stitch
1 strand

raight stitch
2 strands

backstitch
1 strand

straight stitch
2 strands

French knot
1 strand

rows of
stem stitch
2 strands

backstitch
2 strands

backstitch 2 strands
+ fill with rows of
stem stitch 2 strands

135

4· Two Teddies, Front & Back

See projects on page 119

White   436   437   898   347   3347

See project on page 120

White   436   437   898   347   3347

Three Bears, plus Goldilocks

See project on page 121

White 436 437 898 347 3347

7. For the Artistic Bear

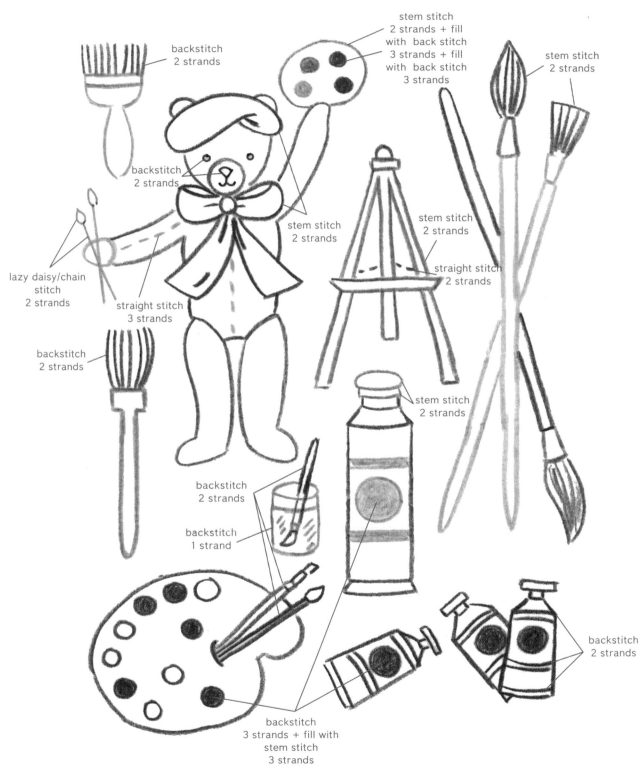

backstitch
2 strands

stem stitch
2 strands + fill
with back stitch
3 strands + fill
with back stitch
3 strands

stem stitch
2 strands

backstitch
2 strands

stem stitch
2 strands

stem stitch
2 strands

straight stitch
2 strands

lazy daisy/chain
stitch
2 strands

straight stitch
3 strands

backstitch
2 strands

stem stitch
2 strands

backstitch
2 strands

backstitch
1 strand

backstitch
2 strands

backstitch
3 strands + fill with
stem stitch
3 strands

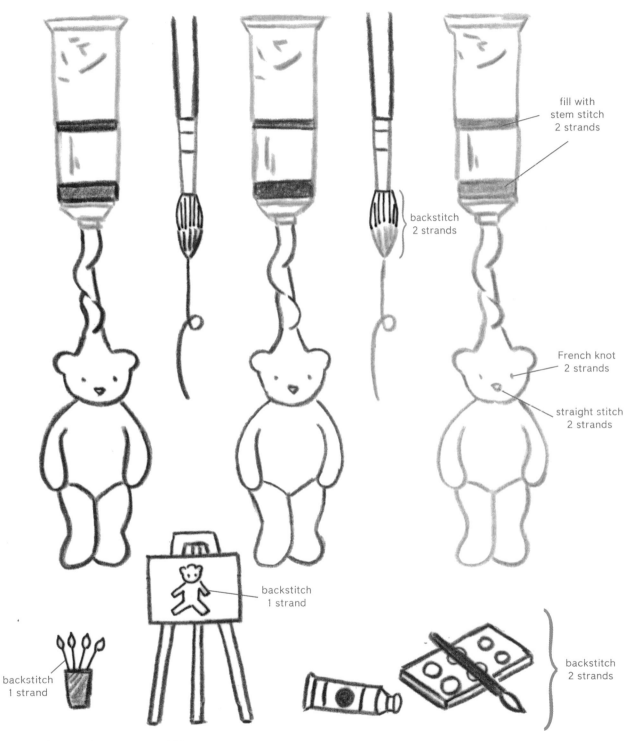

fill with
stem stitch
2 strands

backstitch
2 strands

French knot
2 strands

straight stitch
2 strands

backstitch
1 strand

backstitch
1 strand

backstitch
2 strands

See project on page 122

8

Toy Chest

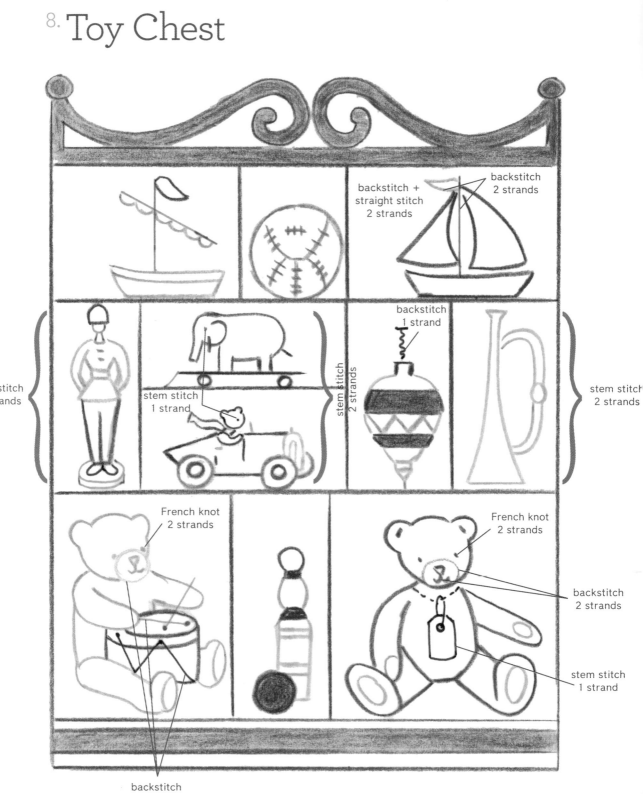

backstitch +
straight stitch
2 strands

backstitch
2 strands

backstitch
1 strand

stem stitch
2 strands

backstitch
3 strands

stem stitch
1 strand

stem stitch
2 strands

French knot
2 strands

French knot
2 strands

backstitch
2 strands

stem stitch
1 strand

backstitch
2 strands

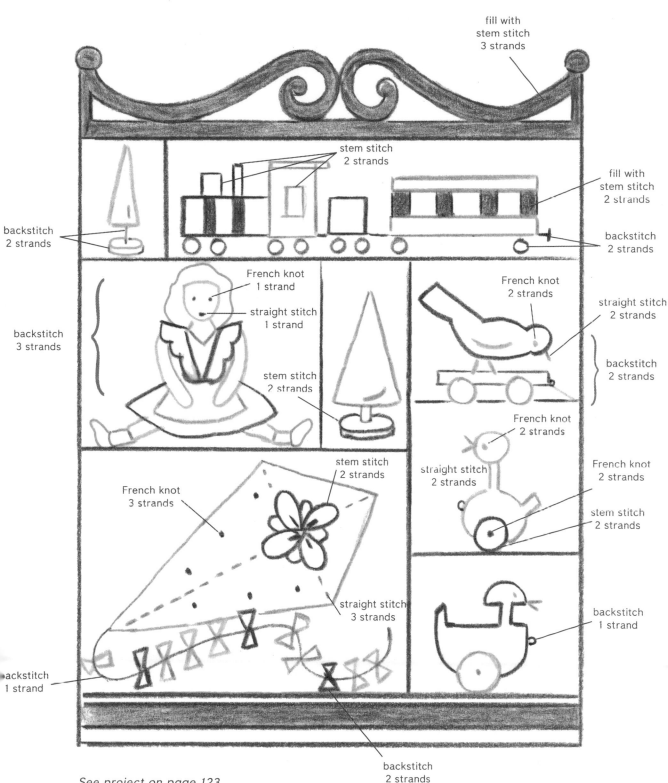

fill with
stem stitch
3 strands

stem stitch
2 strands

fill with
stem stitch
2 strands

backstitch
2 strands

backstitch
2 strands

backstitch
2 strands

French knot
1 strand

straight stitch
1 strand

French knot
2 strands

straight stitch
2 strands

backstitch
3 strands

backstitch
2 strands

stem stitch
2 strands

French knot
2 strands

French knot
2 strands

stem stitch
2 strands

French knot
3 strands

stem stitch
2 strands

straight stitch
2 strands

straight stitch
3 strands

backstitch
1 strand

backstitch
1 strand

backstitch
1 strand

backstitch
2 strands

See project on page 123

145

I Spy a Forest

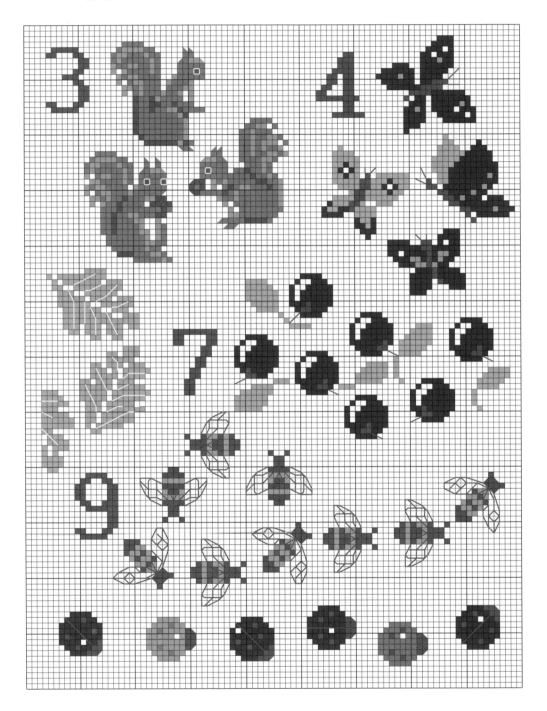

See project on page 124

White   436   437   898   347   3347

Cross-Stitch Teddy Sampler

See project on page 125

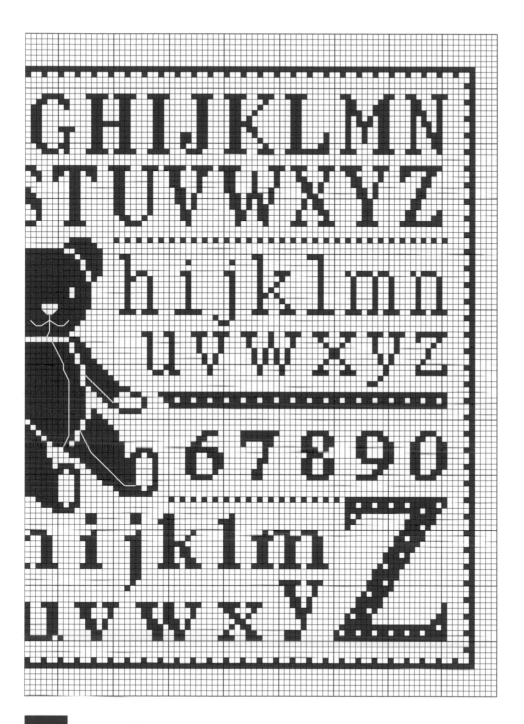

GHIJKLMN
STUVWXYZ
hijklmn
uvwxyz
67890
nijklm
uvwxy Z

347

Furry Family Portraits

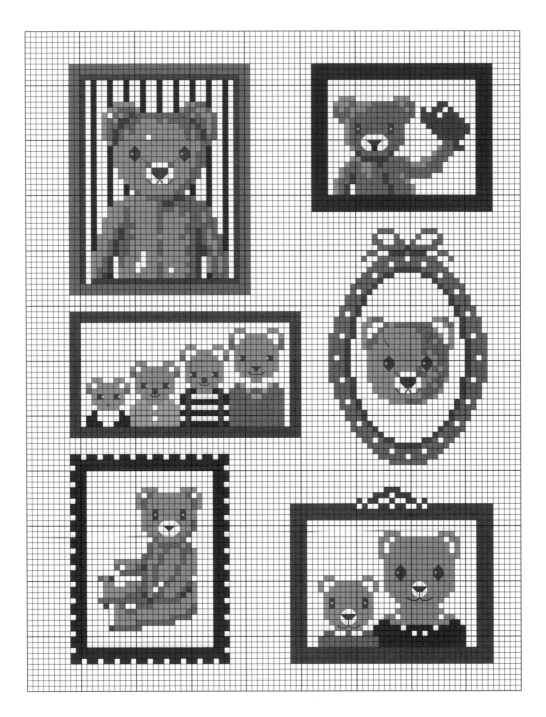

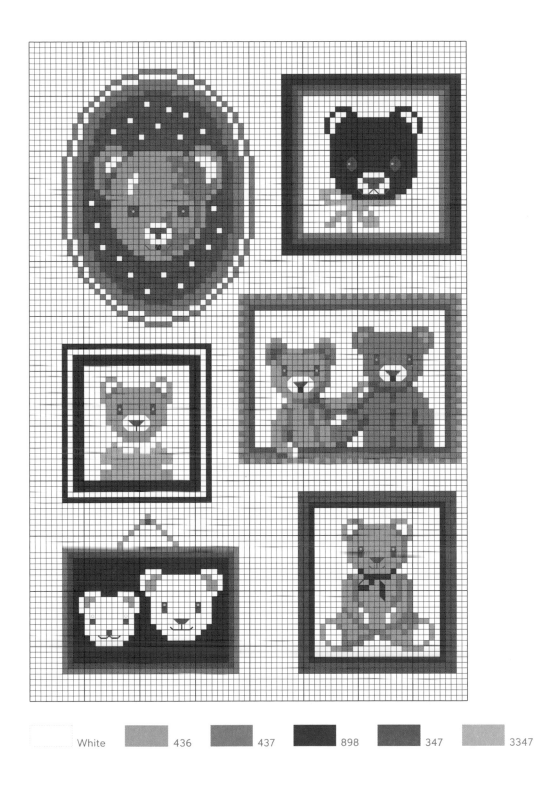

White   436   437   898   347   3347

beautiful
world

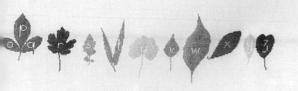

1. Autumn Leaves Coverlet

See motifs on page 174

See project instructions on page 27

2. A Little Birdie Cushion

See motifs on pages 176–177
See project instructions on page 22

3. Bluebird Keepsake Folder

See motifs on page 175

See project instructions on page 31

4. Leaves of Grass Backpack

See motifs on pages 178–179

See project instructions on page 24

See motifs on pages 180–181

6. Nature's Treasures Drawstring Bag

See motifs on page 182

7. Pear Blossom Pencil Case

See motifs on page 184

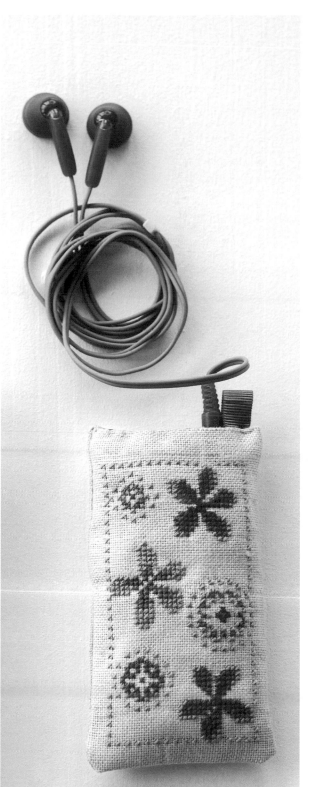

See motifs on page 185

8. Pretty in Pink MP3 Cozy

9. Talking Leaves ABCs

See motifs on pages 186–189

10. Little House Bath Towel

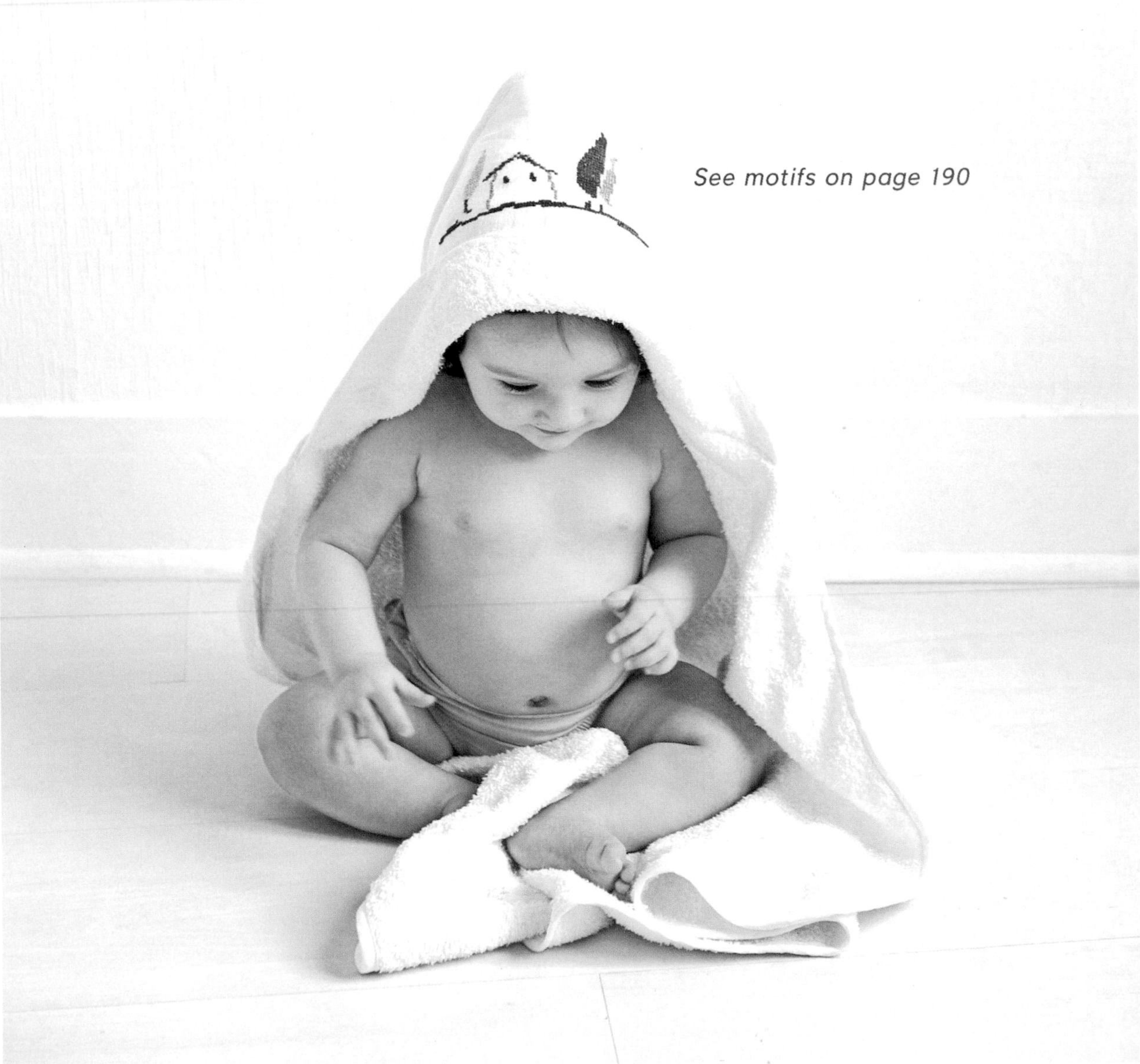

See motifs on page 190

11. Tiny Trees Tee

See motifs on page 190

12. Up, Up & Away Jacket

See motifs on pages 192–193

13. Stardust Baby Organizer

See motifs on pages 194–195

See project instructions on page 23

14· Bring Me the Moon Crib Bumper

See motifs on page 191

15. A Star Is Born Pillow

See motifs on page 196

See project instructions on page 22

16 & 17. Moon & Stars Pullovers

See motifs on page 197

^{18.} Space Explorer ABC

See motifs on pages 198–199

beautiful world motifs

1. Leaves & Tendrils

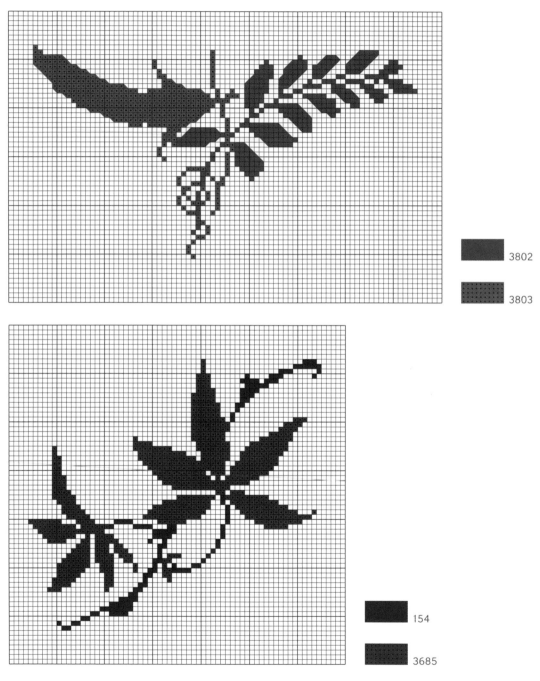

3802

3803

154

3685

See project on page 154

 3808

 3844

 3848

See project on page 156

2. Bird on a Wire

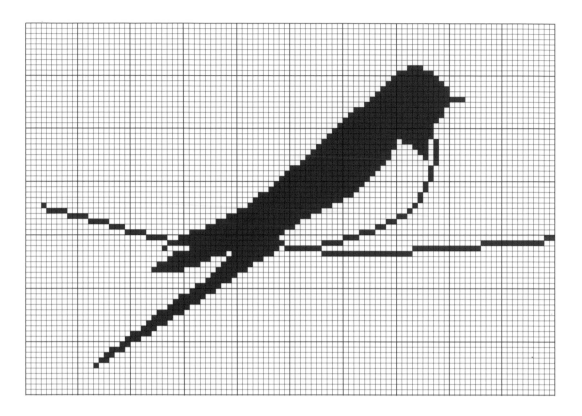

See project on page 155

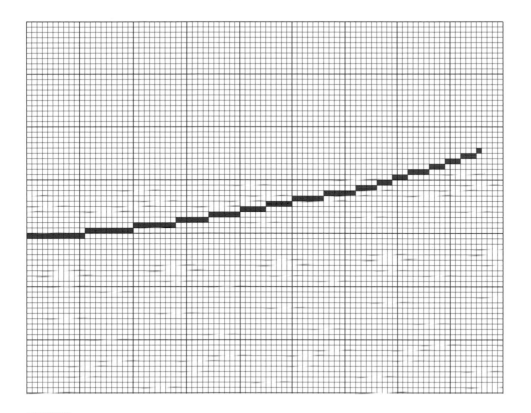

 154

4· Windy Meadow

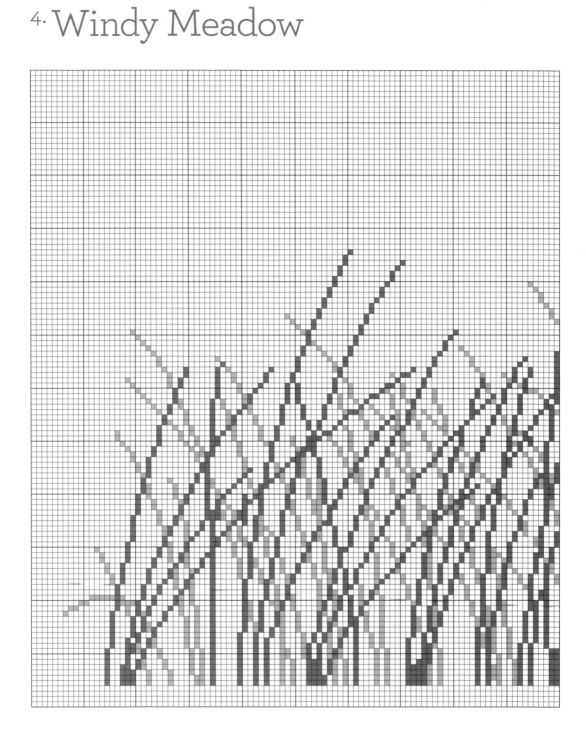

See project on page 157

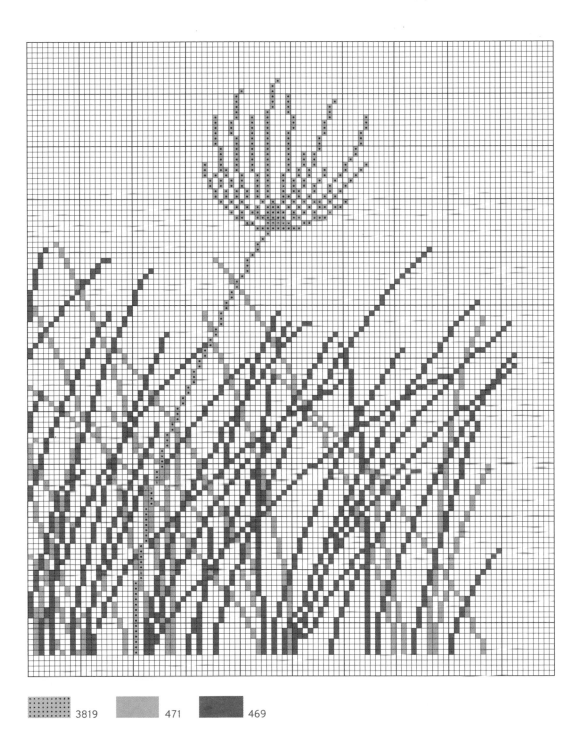

5. Wildflower Garden

See project on page 158

6. Pretty Plumes

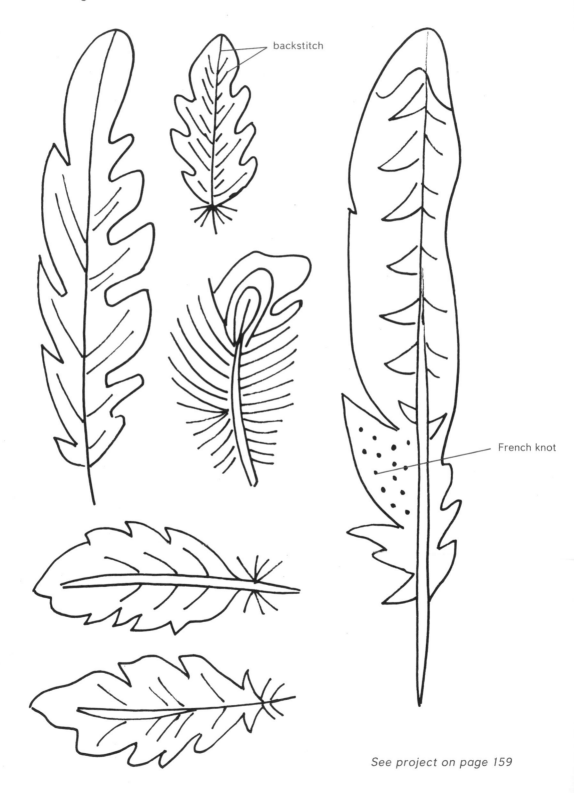

backstitch

French knot

See project on page 159

Horns of Plenty

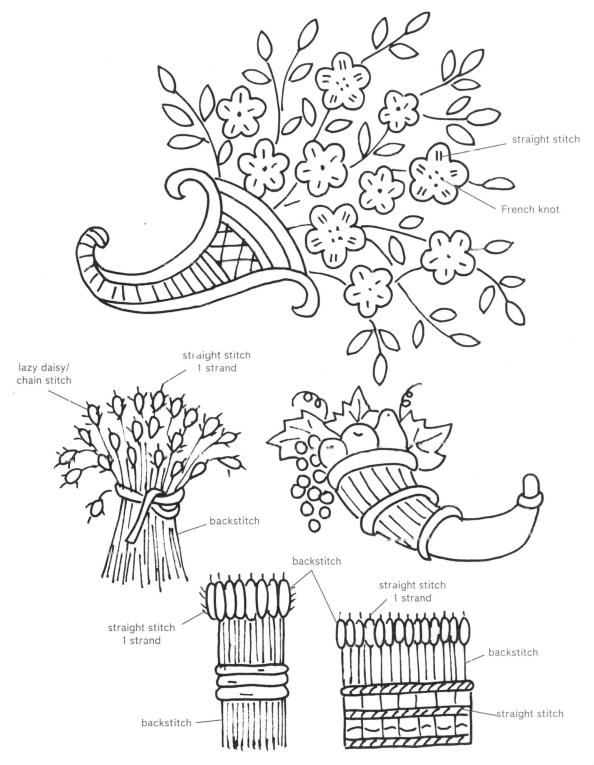

straight stitch

French knot

lazy daisy/
chain stitch

straight stitch
1 strand

backstitch

backstitch

straight stitch
1 strand

straight stitch
1 strand

backstitch

backstitch

straight stitch

backstitch

7. Vine with Pink Flowers

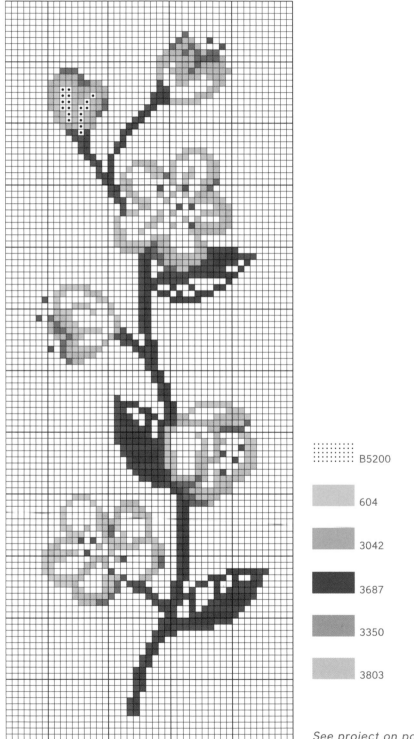

B5200

604

3042

3687

3350

3803

See project on page 160

| | 3835 | | 3806 | | 3805 | | 600 |

See project on page 161

9. Leafy Letters, A through J

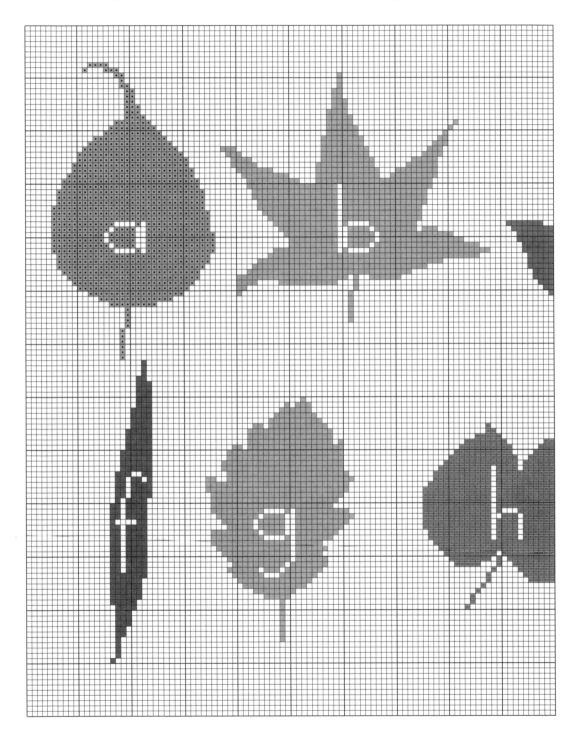

See project on pages 162–163

	3348		3364		3363		522		3052		3051

Leafy Letters, K through Z

See project on pages 162–163

| | 3348 | | 3364 | | 3363 | | 522 | | 3052 | | 3051 |

10. Home Sweet Home

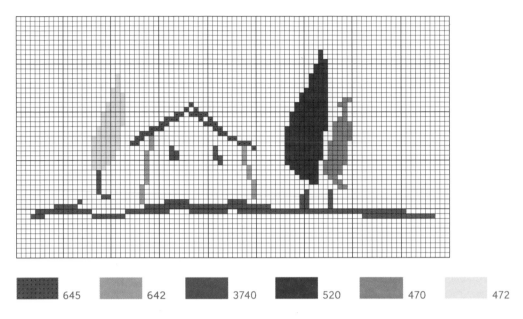

| 645 | 642 | 3740 | 520 | 470 | 472 |

See project on page 164

11. Little Forest

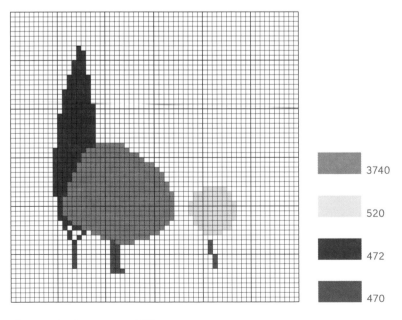

| 3740 | 520 | 472 | 470 |

See project on page 165

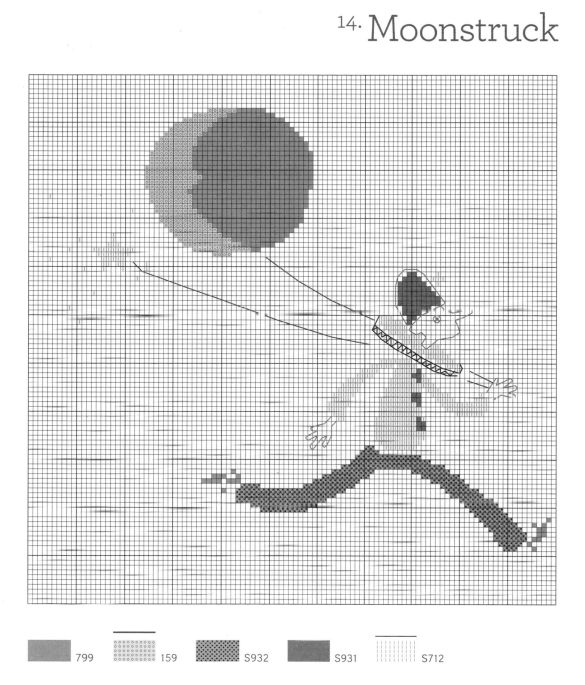

799	159	S932	S931	S712

See project on page 169

Note: The red lines indicate where to use DMC color 159, and the black lines indicate where to use DMC color S712

See project on pages 166–167

E168   3760   3844   471   154

3809   500   522   947

13. A Scattering of Stars

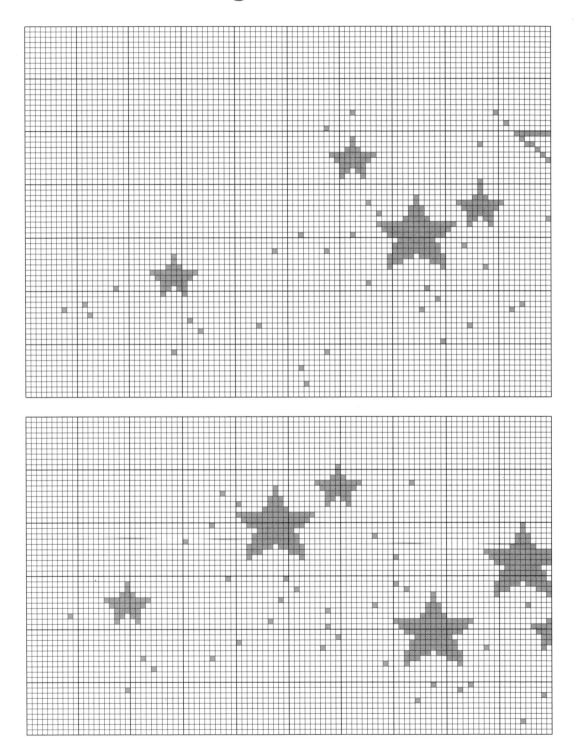

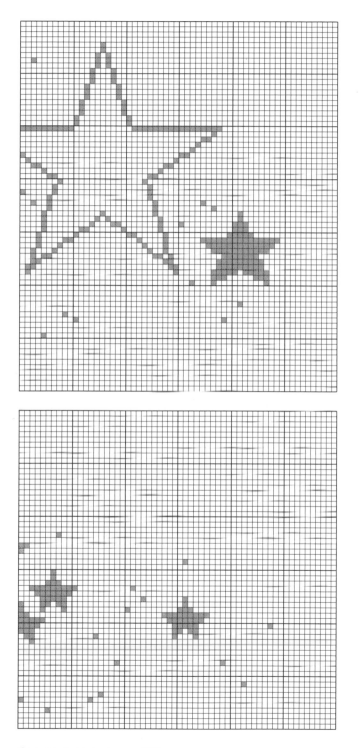

See project on page 168

15· Sun, Moon & Star

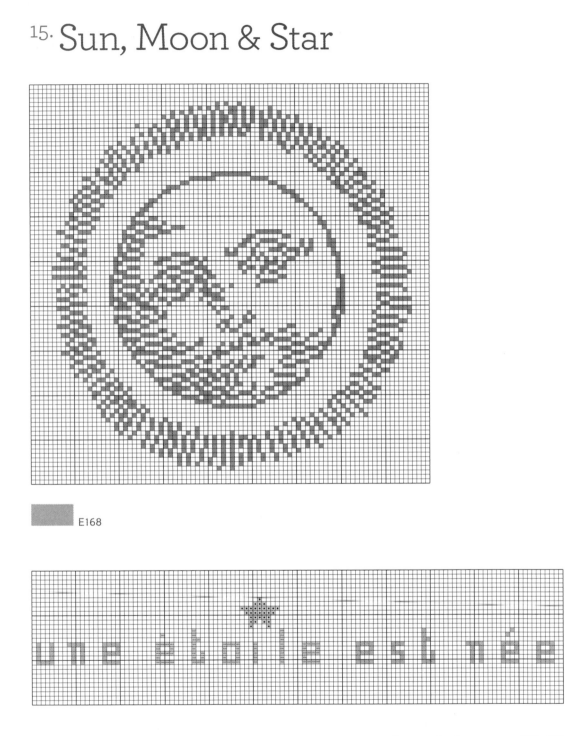

E168

See project on pages 170–171

16 & 17. To the Moon and Beyond

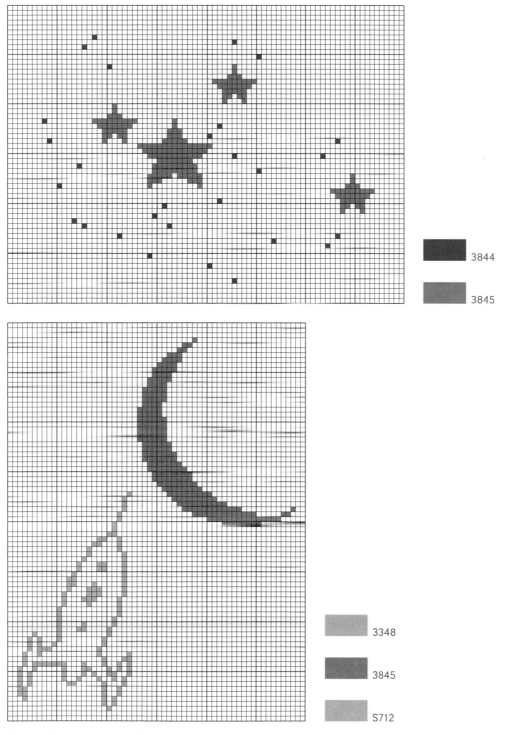

3844

3845

3348

3845

S712

See projects on page 172

18. Rocketship Ride

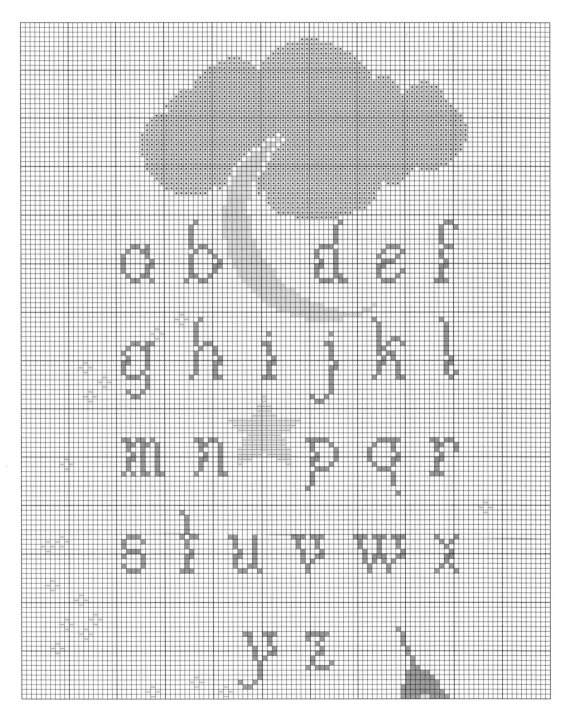

See project on page 173

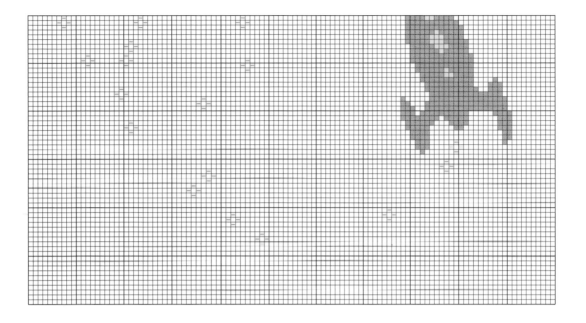

 160

S471

762

S712

E677

belle lettres

1. Delectable Magnets

See motifs on pages 214–217

^{2.} Message on a Button

See motifs on pages 218–219

3. Keep Playing Game Sack

See motif on page 220

4· Call Me Phone Cozy

See motifs on page 221

5. abCD Bag

See motif on page 222

6. Ticket & Passport, Please

See motifs on page 223

See motif on page 224

7. Forget Me Not Sachet

⁸·Beauty & the Beast Pillows

See motifs on pages 225–226

Baby Love Bib

See motif on page 227

See template on page 236

See project instructions on page 26

10. Welcome to My Room!

See motifs on pages 227–229

11. For Hot Chocolate Lovers

See motifs on pages 230–232

12. Pretty Pencils Holder

See motifs on page 233

Color	Code
■	3685
■	600
■	603
■	151
■	3855
■	792
■	310
□	B5200

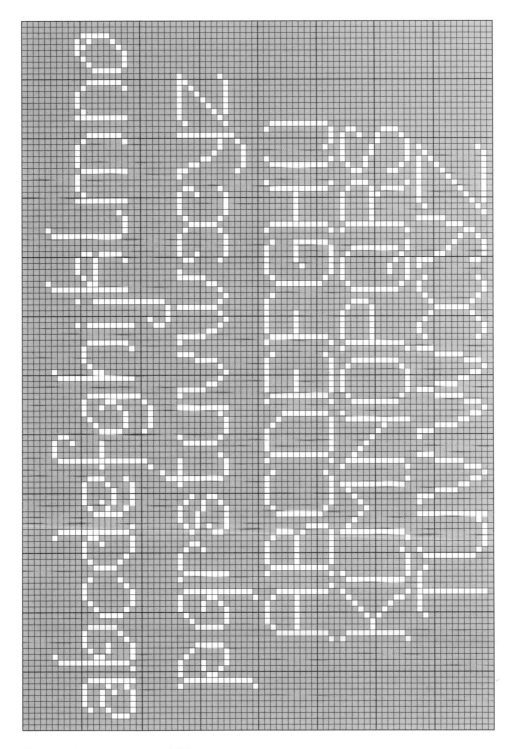

See projects on page 202

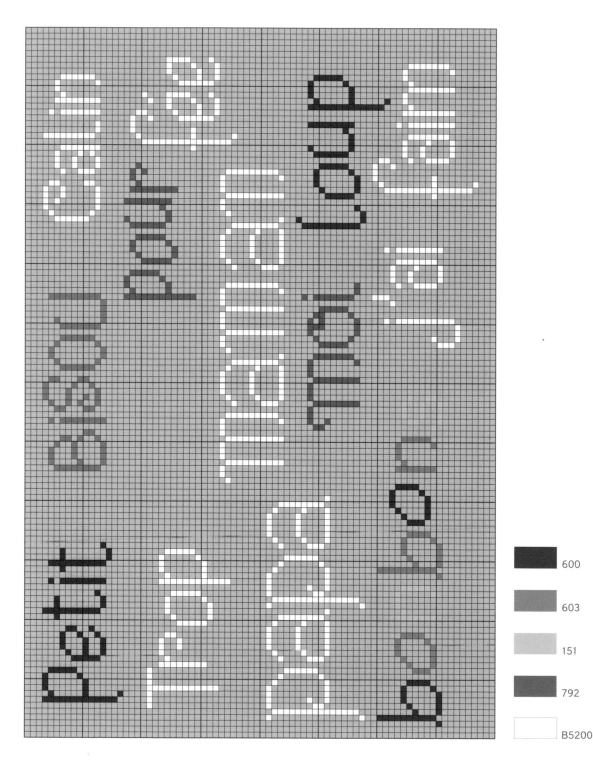

■	600
■	603
■	151
■	792
□	B5200

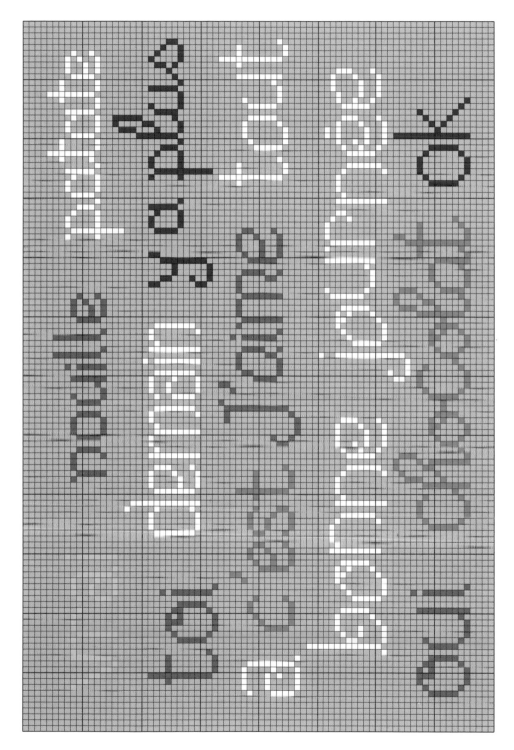

See projects on page 202

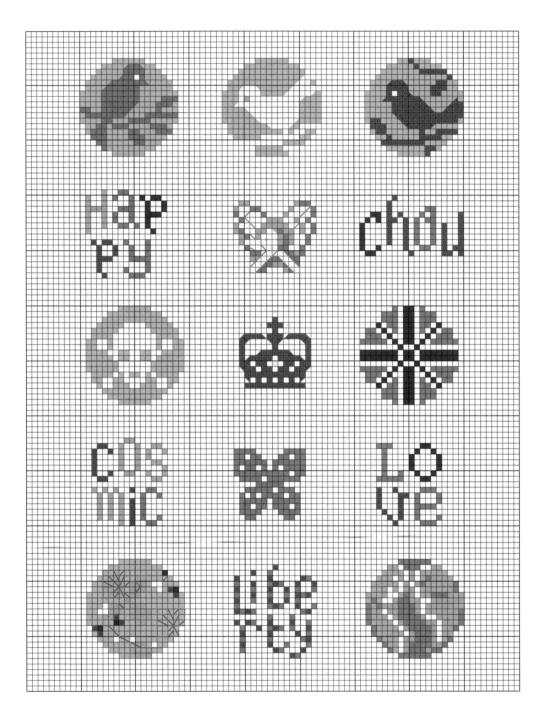

See projects on page 203

B5200 3839 341 3836 3835

603 3805 600 3348

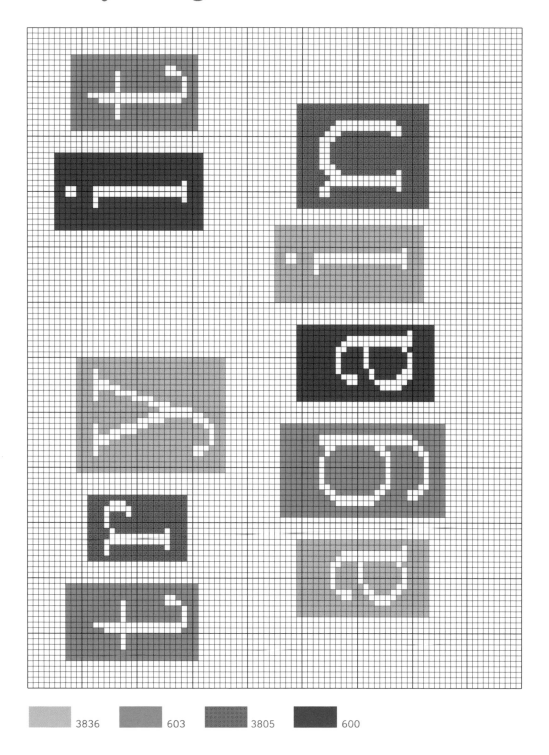

| | 3836 | | 603 | | 3805 | | 600 |

See project on page 204

4. Call Me—Miss You

Symbol	Color
B5200	B5200
3838	3838
3839	3839
341	341
3836	3836
3835	3835
603	603
3805	3805
600	600

See project on page 205

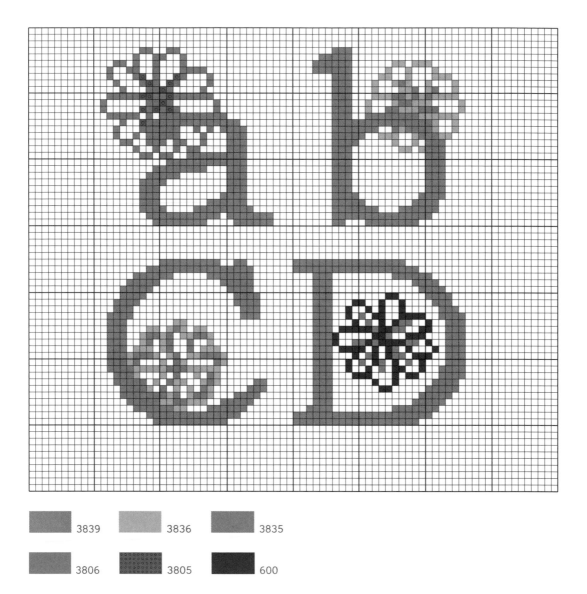

| | 3839 | | 3836 | | 3835 |
| | 3806 | | 3805 | | 600 |

See project on page 206

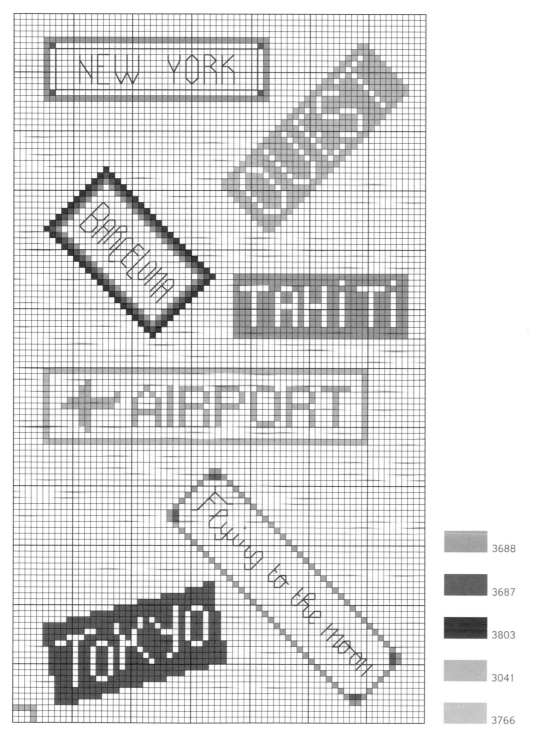

	3688
	3687
	3803
	3041
	3766

See project on page 207

7. Gentle Reminder

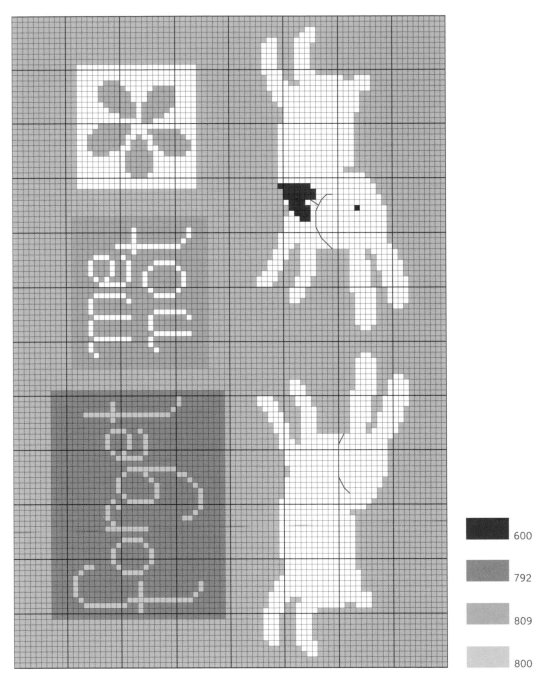

■	600
■	792
■	809
■	800

See project on page 208

3688

See project on page 209

8. The Beast

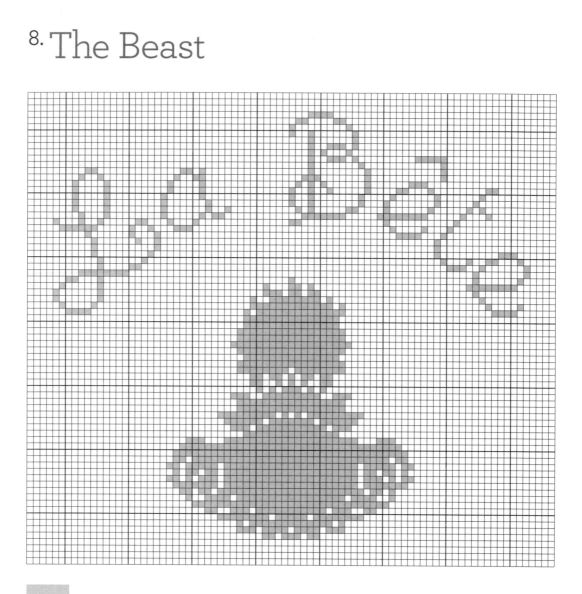

3040

See project on page 210

9. Love with a Flourish

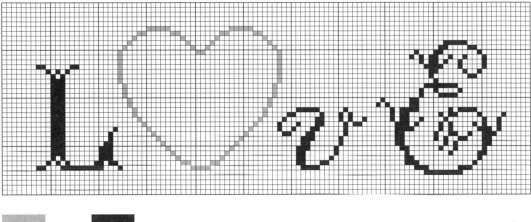

 S712   █ 415

See project on pages 210

10. Come Skip Rope

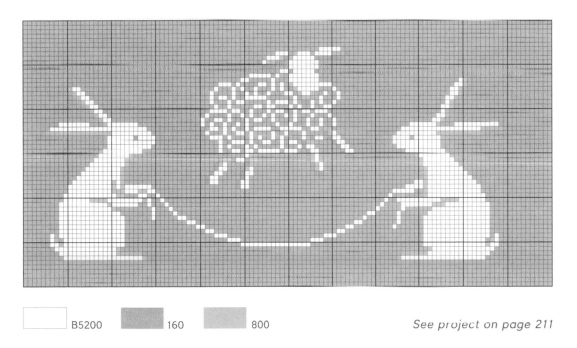

☐ B5200   ▨ 160   ▨ 800

See project on page 211

See project on page 211

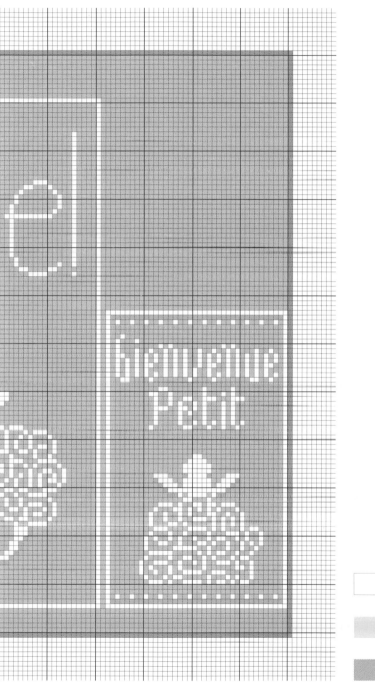

Bienvenue
Petit

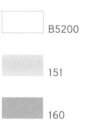

B5200

151

160

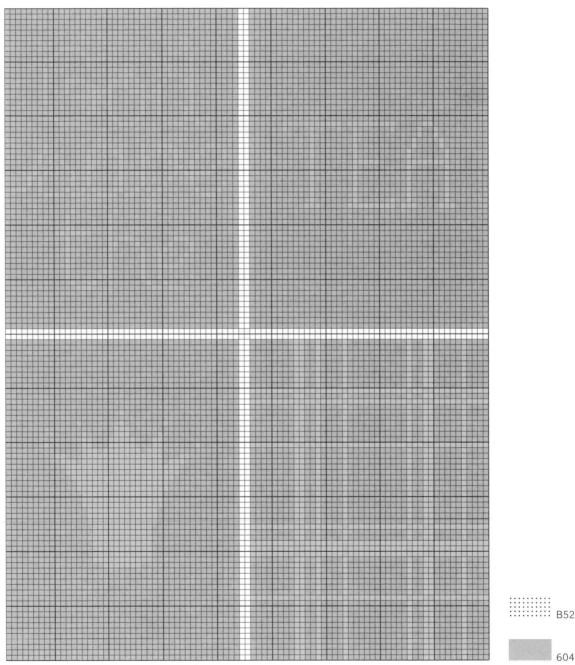

B5200

604

See project on page 212

11. Motif Placement for Hot Chocolate and Tea Canisters

See project on page 212

Delicious

	B5200
	604
	3688
	3687
	3350
	3803
	3041
	3042

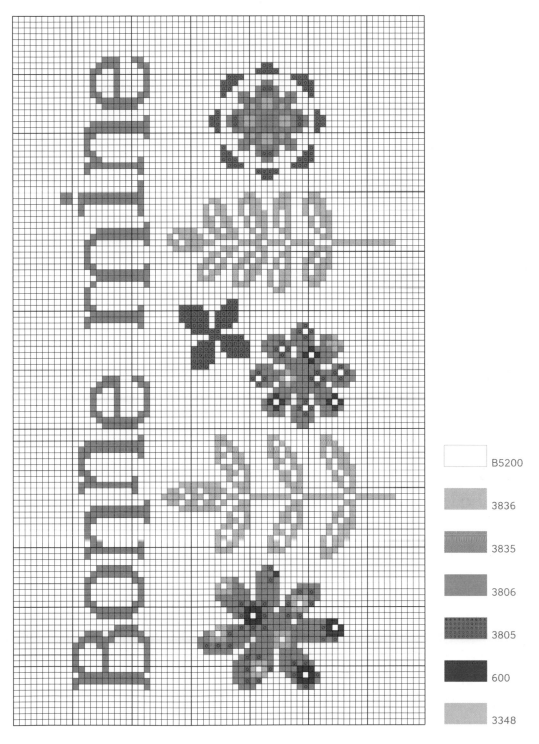

	B5200
	3836
	3835
	3806
	3805
	600
	3348

See project on page 213

Girls' Stuff

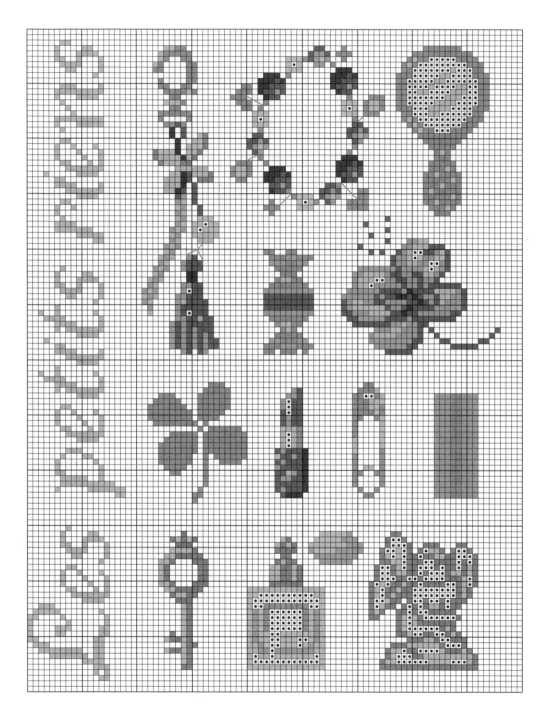

	B5200
	604
	3688
	3687
	3803
	3041
	3042
	161
	3766
	3348

Bib Template

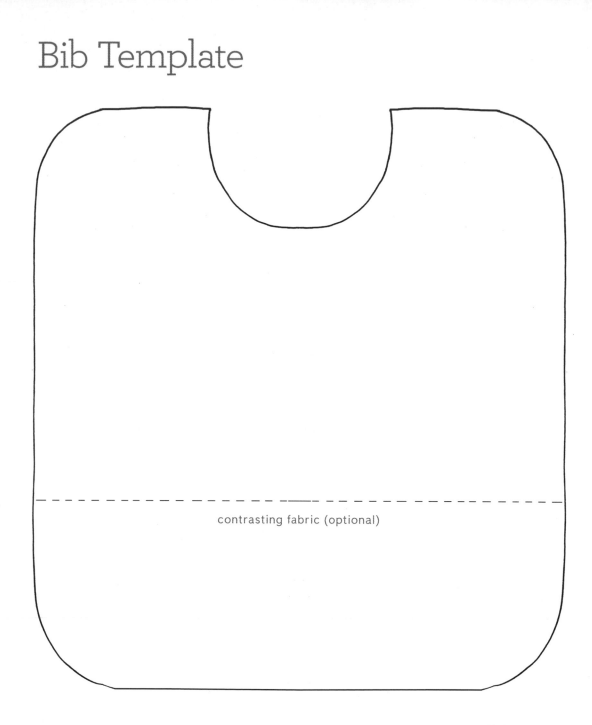

contrasting fabric (optional)

Enlarge 190%

See project on page 210

See motif on page 227

See project instructions on page 26

craft supplies

A.C. MOORE

www.acmoore.com

1-800-ACMOORE

HOBBY LOBBY

www.hobbylobby.com

For mail order or online purchasing:

www.craftsetc.com

1-800-888-0321

JO-ANN

www.joann.com

1-888-739-4120

MICHAELS

www.michaels.com

1-800-MICHAELS (1-800-642-4235)

embroidery floss

ANCHOR

www.coatsandclark.com

800-648-1479

To purchase online:

www.yarncollection.com

1-877-292-0062

CustomerService@YarnCollection.com

THE CARON COLLECTION

www.caron-net.com

203-381-9999

CRESCENT COLLECTION

www.crescentcolours.com

1-888-9-THREAD

DMC

www.dmc-usa.com

973-589-0606

dmcusa@dmcus.com

THE GENTLE ART

www.thegentleart.com

614-855-8346

KREINIK

www.kreinik.com

1-800-537-2166

info@kreinik.com

RAINBOW GALLERY

www.rainbowgallery.com

email@rainbowgallery.com

WEEKS DYE WORKS

www.weeksdyeworks.com

877-OVERDYE

contact@weeksdyeworks.com

YLI

www.ylicorp.com

803-985-3100

ylicorp@ylicorp.com

aida cloth

CHARLES CRAFT

charlescraft.com

973-589-0606

dmcusa@dmcus.com

DMC

www.dmc-usa.com

973-589-0606

dmcusa@dmcus.com

ZWEIGART

www.zweigart.com

732-562-8888

info@zweigart.com

fabric transfer paper

AVERY

www.avery.com

1-800-GO AVERY (800 467 8379)

EPSON

www.epson.com

800-873-7766

HP

www.shopping.hp.com

888-999-4747

floss conversion chart

The numbers given in this book refer to the colors of DMC embroidery floss.

Here are numbers for the closest color matches of other major brands.

DMC	Anchor	Kreinik
Blanc	002	8000, 7124
B5200	001	8000
150	59	1057
151	23	no match
154	873	634
159	120	no match
160	176	no match
161	122	no match
168	398	8073
310	403	8050
317	400	8086, 8075, 875
318	399	824, 8084
341	117	524, 5203
347	1025	117
415	398	8084
436	1045	7175
437	362	7175
451	233	no match
469	267	4215
470	267	no match
471	265	4213
472	253	4212
500	683	4167, 4067
520	862	4077, 4206
522	860	4076, 4204, 434
600	78	1057
602	63	1055
603	52	1054
604	55	1105
605	74	1033
640	903	7025
642	392	7024
644	830	4073, 403, 433

DMC	Anchor	Kreinik
645	273	8055
677	886	7173, 2013, 732
712	926	7124, 712, 723
762	234	8073, 8053
792	177	no match
799	136	5093
800	159	544, 5053
809	175	5012
815	43	1119
822	390	7172, 7012, 403
898	360	7136
927	848	4096, 444
928	274	4093, 543, 513
930	1035	5057
931	921	5055
932	920	553, 525
938	381	4206
947	330	2066
988	243	4034
3041	871	634, 6126
3042	870	6124, 633
3051	681	4216, 4206
3052	262	434, 4215
3347	266	no match
3348	264	no match
3350	59	1055
3363	262	434
3364	260	4214, 4204
3371	382	7166
3685	1028	1107
3687	68	1105, 116
3688	66	116, 115
3740	873	6127, 634

DMC	Anchor	Kreinik
3760	169	5105
3765	170	5105
3766	167	553, 534
3781	904	7135
3802	1019	1205, 1107, 6207
3803	972	1105
3805	62	1055
3806	62	1054
3808	1068	4046, 5105
3809	1066	4044, 5105
3810	1066	5104, 534
3819	923	no match
3834	100	6127
3835	98	6126, 6116
3836	90	6116, 6114
3838	177	5204
3839	176	5204, 525
3844	410	no match
3845	1089	no match
3848	1074	536, 4044
3855	311	7174

index

Note: Page numbers in italics indicate motifs.

HILLSBORO PUBLIC LIBRARIES
Hillsboro, OR
Member of Washington County
COOPERATIVE LIBRARY SERVICES